THIS

STRANGE

VISIBLE

AIR

OTHER BOOKS BY SHARON BUTALA

FICTION

Country of the Heart

Queen of the Headaches (stories)

The Gates of the Sun

Luna

Fever (stories)

Upstream

The Fourth Archangel

The Garden of Eden

Real Life (stories)

Wild Rose

Zara's Dead

Season of Fury and Wonder (stories)

NONFICTION

Harvest

The Perfection of the Morning: An Apprenticeship in Nature

Coyote's Morning Cry: Meditations and Dreams from a Life in Nature

Wild Stone Heart: Apprenticed to the Fields

Old Man on His Back

Lilac Moon: Dreaming of the Real West

The Girl in Saskatoon: A Meditation on Friendship, Memory, and Murder

Where I Live Now

This Strange Visible Air: Essays on Aging and the Writing Life

THIS

Essays on

STRANGE

Aging and the Writing Life

VISIBLE

Sharon Butala

AIR

Freehand Books acknowledges the financial support for its publishing program provided by the Canada Council for the Arts and the Alberta Media Fund, and by the Government of Canada through the Canada Book Fund.

 Canada Council for the Arts Conseil des Arts du Canada   Alberta Government Canada

Freehand Books
515–815 1st Street SW   Calgary, Alberta   T2P 1N3
www.freehand-books.com

Book orders: UTP Distribution
5201 Dufferin Street   Toronto, Ontario   M3H 5T8
Telephone: 1-800-565-9523   Fax: 1-800-221-9985
utpbooks@utpress.utoronto.ca utpdistribution.com

Library and Archives Canada Cataloguing in Publication
Title: This strange visible air : essays on aging and the writing life /
by Sharon Butala.
Names: Butala, Sharon, 1940– author.
Identifiers: Canadiana (print) 20210241381 | Canadiana (ebook)
20210241535 | ISBN 9781988298962 (softcover) | ISBN 9781988298979 (EPUB)
| ISBN 9781988298986 (PDF)
Subjects: LCSH: Butala, Sharon, 1940– | CSH: Authors, Canadian
(English)—20th century—Biography. | CSH: Women authors, Canadian
(English)—20th century—Biography. | LCSH: Older authors—Canada—
Biography. | LCSH: Older women—Canada—Biography. | LCSH: Old age. |
LCGFT: Autobiographies.
Classification: LCC PS8553.U6967 Z46 2021 | DDC C813/.54—dc23

Edited by Naomi K. Lewis
Cover design by Grace Cheong
Cover image © Don White / iStock.com
Author photo by Jennifer Chipperfield
Printed on FSC® certified paper and bound in Canada by Marquis

MIX
Paper from responsible sources
FSC
www.fsc.org   FSC® C103567

FOR

SEAN

CONTENTS

9   *Against Ageism*

17 *Open Your Eyes*

31 *Cold Ankles*

43 *Storage*

59 *A Life in Friends*

81 *This Strange Visible Air*

87 *Passing Through*

95 *Perceptible Light*

105 *Lettuce or Things I Can't Do Now That I'm Old*

109 *Inglorious on the LRT*

129 *Sharon Deals with the Problem of Evil*

143 *The Murder Remains Unsolved*

163 *Vanished Without a Trace*

193 *Doing the Right Thing*

213 *On the Pandemic*

229 WORKS CITED   231 ACKNOWLEDGEMENTS

AGAINST AGEISM

On the day my husband died, I was two weeks short of my sixty-seventh birthday, and I thought that once I got through the terrible grief and the distress of having to leave the rolling grasslands of southern Saskatchewan, where I'd lived for thirty-three years, for Calgary, I would still have many years ahead of me in which to have a wonderful new life. Glimmering faintly on the horizon were art galleries, concert halls, the opera, professional theatre, new, like-minded friends, and, maybe, someday, even a new relationship. But what I didn't have a clue about was that I was soon to be *old*, or what being *old* would mean to my dreams and desires. While dreading old age with every fibre, I was at the same time in full denial that it would ever happen to me, and, so, was shocked down to the soles of my feet when it did.

On the day old age strikes, our host is pouring drinks on the terrace; the hot tub is bubbling, and the sunlit mountains shine in their beauty around us. But our hearts are numb with permanently thwarted desire, our throats choked with longing for things we will never have again, and our future, we are sure, is too bleak to contemplate. We stare in terror into the abyss, and ask ourselves: *Who am I now?*

How I struggled in the face of this transition, as my body changed and grew more fragile no matter what I did to stop it, and as younger people started ignoring me, or treating me as if I were a not-very-smart, obstinate child. And due to my less robust physicality, and my new single status, I was having to cut away, one by one, the things I used to do: bike riding, cross-country skiing, two-hour-long hikes, adventurous trips, and most after-dark outings. How on earth was I to find this "wonderful" new life?

What I was facing is ubiquitous, but fairly new in the span of human history. In the past, when we all died much younger, old people were fairly rare, caused little trouble, and, in Western society, were easily ignored. But today, an extraordinary six million Canadians are senior citizens. Never before in North American history have older adults formed such a large proportion of the population. And since women tend to live longer than men, the older the age group, the higher the percentage of females. Women like me, now in our late seventies and alone for the first time in many years, find ourselves socializing almost exclusively with women, and rarely meet a single male (whether we are interested in finding one or not) or even a male who isn't a family member. We have to rethink what we value, because so much of our lives have reached fruition: working to fulfill career goals or toward buying the dream house or country cottage, meeting new partners, starting new families, getting doctorates, and even the pleasure of living securely as respected, useful elders within our own multi-aged clans, none of which I ever achieved, having come out of poverty, put myself and a husband through university, and then retreated, for the last thirty-three years, to a second husband's at-first hardscrabble ranch in the middle of nowhere. I assume an audience mostly more privileged than I've been.

But, nonetheless, even I find myself, along with the much-maligned baby boomers (I'm six years older than the oldest baby boomer) forced to find meaning in places we might not have bothered with when we were younger and half of a couple: solitude, friendship, watching birds and animals, hobbies, keeping-the-wolf-from-the-door part-time jobs, and, if we are so inclined, a closer following of music, painting, and theatre. The increase in time spent alone can be a soul-wrenching shift that forces us to ask ourselves in dismay and fear: *What matters now?*

WE OLDER PEOPLE don't want to spend the many good years ahead of us staring out the window at a busy world rushing past that no longer has any place for us. Yet we have fallen victim to the Age of Invisibility. On the one hand, everyone around me prefers to ignore old people, and, on the other, treats this large and important demographic as a problem to be solved, thinking in terms of pensions and income levels, health care and housing needs, and recently, loneliness, rather than as a resource from which the benefits of experience-based, thoughtful advice might flow, to enrich our country.

The first and worst thing both for us old people, and for our society, is the staggering ageism everywhere we turn. This societal belief, whether frankly articulated or merely an unspoken assumption, and in which we too are often complicit, is that old people are useless, a drain on society, and an inferior form of humanity. Every senior has experienced the disrespect, the rudeness, and outright dismissal from people younger than us, until we begin to feel that staying locked in our homes is the only bearable route, or else moving to gated retirement communities limited to others like us. Take restaurants, for example: the waitstaff, usually very young, always turn first to the youngest person at the table, and last to, well, me, when it should be the other way around. And I, small, visibly old, and female, find getting served anywhere with a lineup requires a loud, authoritative voice, and sometimes my most powerful glare designed to terrify.

For the most part, nobody thinks the old person in any group has anything pertinent, useful, or interesting to say, and the style of the old, unfortunately, contributes to this notion. It isn't just that we no longer look fabulous and our bodies won't allow us to dress like Beyoncé or TV's scarily smartly-dressed *The Good Wife*, but also, for the most part, we aren't instantly articulate and fast-talking, but instead choose to take time to think first, to speak slowly, to reach into our vast well of experience to find an apt example or a learning. Young people are annoyed by slowness; they haven't time to get a grip on the idea so carefully formulated; they laugh at the uncool word choice, and at what they think is our failure to understand *their* new world. And they suspect us of being able only to lecture, or to provide only bland, irritating homilies.

Society judges us in terms of the values, abilities, and desires of the young. By such standards we old can only fail. We are no longer part of the ruling culture of youth with its emphasis on physical beauty, agility, and litheness, and on mental quickness: the celebration of competitive athletes, for instance, and pop music with its fabulous-looking if plasticized stars, the fashion industry, and the glib, speedy, ill-mannered chatterers on TV and radio. But I insist that we are not merely failed copies of the young; we are a whole new class of citizens, and it is time for all of us, the young and the old, to create a new framework out of which to view older adults, to genuinely honour us, and to begin to celebrate and use the virtually unique gifts the elderly have to offer.

First, we elderly have to stop denigrating ourselves with comments such as "I'm just an old fool; I'm only a little old lady." Second, we have to start teaching the young to show automatic respect for the elderly, not because they are feeble and dumb, but because they know more than the young do, and have seen more and understand more about the world. At the same time, we should start inculcating some of the values other cultures rightly demand — boards, government councils, and decision-making bodies should include elders, not as token gestures, but as a matter of course (as many First Nations, Inuit, and Métis councils and organizations do). Here's another suggestion: make specific places for us to contribute at the beginning, not at the end, of a conference, and then *listen* to us. We should be on school and hospital boards as well as municipal councils and municipally operated community centres. We could begin a wide-ranging and concerted societal effort to stop all forms of ageism.

Wouldn't it be great to see the young and charismatic working hand in hand with the elderly and experienced, each influencing the other? What we elderly have been through has taught us what we often don't even realize we know, and what the young certainly don't know. We older adults have a lot of work to do too, and, in my experience, most of us are already making hard-won changes to the ways we experience and think about our lives.

We elders can become, as author Theodore Roszak put it, "agents for change," which is possible by virtue of our very numbers. Currently, the aged are viewed as a large coherent group, even though we range in age by thirty years easily, as well as by class, education, degree of affluence, race, sexual orientation, political and religious ideas, and whether able-bodied or not. (I heard on the radio recently a woman who, at sixty, was referred to as "elderly.") How many of us really expect to spend our last days as we appear in insurance ads, sitting in bathing suits gazing at the sunset on a faraway beach? How many of us can afford insurance? As agents for change, we could start by working to rid both ourselves and society of the pernicious ideas that make up ageism, and that allow the media and individuals to get away with derogatory remarks about us, which we wouldn't permit racists, sexists, homophobes, or antisemites to get away with either in print, TV, radio, or real life. For example, I've heard nasty comments more than once on the radio about old women tucking tissues up their sleeves or down their bosoms, and how disgusting that is, remarks stemming out of a horror of getting old. But most women's everyday garments don't have pockets anymore, and (according to an ear, nose, and throat specialist) nasal secretions thicken with age, accounting for the constant need for a tissue.

I have considered launching a relentless but civil letter-writing campaign to the perpetrators, some quite unthinking and others deliberate and cruel in their mockery, every time I hear a speaker on the radio make an ageist remark, or see stereotypes about the old on television, or read condescending remarks about us in magazines and newspapers. I want to raise societal awareness of the untruths of most such assumptions, and the immense harm being done by them — a new kind of the "consciousness-raising" that my friends and I learned during the Second Wave of Feminism in the sixties and seventies — one that recognizes that, as we age, we find within ourselves a stronger kindness, and a compassion in daily life that, for us, outweighs legal, economic, and political considerations, which too often are the most powerful imperatives in decision-making and that further polarize our society.

WHAT ROLE CAN older adults play in society? I think we, the elderly, are formulating it even now. We must take the lead, because only those who are citizens of that kingdom truly understand it. Our days of quick wit, instant insights, and brilliant feats of memory so highly valued by the young *are* over, but our real intelligence and, especially, our true wisdom, which is partly dispassion and partly compassion, have expanded vastly in ways the young can't even imagine.

In the last ten years I have gone from profound grief, bafflement, and near despair to a growing sense that I'm getting closer to knowing what life really is. I began in a log house in the Saskatchewan bush, taught at the University of

Saskatchewan, spent years as a mother and a city woman, then spent many more as horseback-riding cattle rancher, and travelled widely, published more than twenty books, had five plays produced, and found myself fetching up, possibly finally, in a condo in Calgary. I am stunned and heartened by this accounting, and sometimes, though rarely, even joyful. Laughter begins to seem the best response — not the rage of the young — but a measure of delighted laughter. I am coming to understand what I personally need to live out these last years — who knows how many — with a measure of peace, with serious pleasure in things I hardly noticed when I was young, to live more in the now than I have ever done, and to look backward at my long life as if it were a lovely dream, even the pain, the endless injustice, even the horror. I heard myself say the other day to my own amazement, "I have had a wonderful life." What young or middle-aged person can say that and then laugh out loud in amused surprise at having seen something true, finally?

After I've finished the necessary examination of my life, knowing that living in the past is a trap, death itself, and that my future is limited and probably not going to be glorious, and finally accepting my age rather than denying it, I have found myself quite inadvertently savouring the moment, focusing on it, not as the spiritual discipline known as mindfulness but as a natural development in and of the state of being old. Through this attention to the moment, true joy in the wonders of being alive in the world, so rare otherwise in adulthood, finally come. As Theodore Roszak said, back in 1998, "If wisdom means anything, it means the ability to see through the illusions of youth."

OPEN YOUR EYES

"Loneliness is the first thing which God's eye nam'd not good."
John Milton (1608–1674)

6:30 a.m. Yesterday was . . . Monday . . . so this must be Tuesday. Click on the lamp, throw back the duvet, stand. On the way to the bathroom, turn on the computer. Turn up the thermostat, lift the blind: Snow? No snow? Push the button to start the coffeemaker you readied last night. Put on your dressing gown and thick socks. Take the morning's pills with last night's glass of stale water. Check for email. The coffeemaker pings; pour a cup, get back into bed, open the current book.

Read while you sip the coffee. The house is silent; outside, the street is silent, will be until the school buses disgorge noisy children to the school across the way. When the cup is nearly empty, the coffee cold, put down the book, go back to the computer, sit down; call up the file you're working on. Stare at the screen.

It's an essay on loneliness.

Old people are expert on this subject. You might even say it goes with the condition of being old. And sadly, for the most part anything that can be said on the subject is obvious and has already been said ten thousand times by everyone from the lonely themselves to city planners, poets, sociologists, theologians, psychoanalysts, and your next-door neighbour. And we all know, too, or at some juncture or other in our lives we discover, that loneliness is, in our North American world, ubiquitous and thought to be caused by the cult of the individual, the nuclear family, the rise of narcissism, the worship of celebrity, globalization, and late-stage capitalism itself. As an old person, I live in the midst of a community of loneliness — admittedly a contradiction in terms: how do the lonely make a community and remain lonely? But somehow, we manage it.

Only when you decide to write an essay on this again newly trendy subject, after having some long, heightened personal experience with loneliness, do you discover what a voluminous literature exists about it, from modern expert studies completed by government departments, to personal essays going back to sixteenth-century Michel de Montaigne, although his is called "On Solitude," much like psychiatrist Anthony Storr's popular book, *Solitude: A Return to the Self.*

Both books conclude (as we might expect) that solitude is good, while loneliness is bad, and that loneliness is a complex emotion, state, and condition. In the hands of philosophers, the subject is almost beyond your (my, anyway) ability to understand, and their deep probing examines, as is inevitable, the related concepts of grief, sorrow, depression, and homesickness, too. In old people, homesickness is usually a longing for a home that no longer exists, or for a home that, even if one stood in the middle of it, wouldn't feel like the longed-for home anyway. And that would be loneliness.

I am surprised to find that friends my own age, the elderly, who take part in a number of activities, so are out of their homes and with congenial people often, still claim to be lonely. Some of us can spend three to five days completely alone, the phone not even ringing unless it is the cursed telephone marketers, no one knocking on the door, and having to go to the grocery store or the post office or even to the doctor just to have a human conversation.

When I was eight years old, I lived in a village in central Saskatchewan (north of most of the world), and attended a one-room school with Grades 1 to 8. On a hot Friday afternoon in June, when everybody tends to slack off, we girls were wearing summer dresses, and our young teacher sent us outside, around to the back of the school to our baseball diamond. There we all were — somehow, despite our different ages, sizes, and sexes — organized to play softball.

I remember playing for a while. I didn't enjoy sports, wasn't athletic, was a tiny child, and was bored, because there were double the required numbers to make up the teams, and I was, of course, among the last to be chosen. When my turn to play finally came, I knew that I would strike out, and that my teammates would berate me for it. After a while, I wandered away from the game around to the front of the empty school and sat down, alone, on the wooden steps leading inside. Eventually, a sweaty older girl came panting around the side of the building looking for a drink of water. Seeing me, she hesitated, and asked why I was sitting there by myself. I probably said that I didn't want to play ball — our mother didn't allow us to shrug our shoulders or say "I dunno" when she spoke to us, so I would have said something. She went inside, and came rushing back out, swiping water from her chin, and ran back to the game.

She must have told the teacher where I was. "Oh," the teacher must have said, and knowing I wouldn't get into mischief, seeing no other reason to insist I come back, left me there. This happened just after World War II, when experienced teachers were still in short supply. Probably a teenager herself, with zero knowledge of child psychology, she likely couldn't be bothered engaging me in a conversation about why I left. And so I sat alone, listening to the crack of the bat on the ball and the cries of my classmates floating to me through the warm spring air over the roof of the school.

But mostly I remember sitting there, elbows on my knees, chin resting on my palms, and feeling . . . what? Peaceful and quiet, I think, aware of myself as alone in a wide, noisy world, enjoying my distance from it, if also feeling the creeping approach of loneliness, the boundary between solitude and loneliness being permeable and unstable. I remember that after a while, I got up off the steps and went back to the game. I remember — I think — that I found the teacher playing in the infield, sweat trickling down her temple, and when she glanced at me, her expression rested somewhere between annoyed and indifferent. I already knew that look from my mother, and was, by this time — at eight — girded against it.

Seventy years later, I still recall this incident, although without the shame I once associated with it — my peculiarities, my sullenness — as cementing my status as a loner and a pursuer of solitude. (Along the way, I would also become recalcitrant.) And yet, now, I, along with those friends my age who admit to suffering from loneliness, do everything that remains within our power (without being able to bring the dead back to life, or cure our Parkinson's, arthritis, or congestive heart failure) to relieve or dispel it. To tell yourself that everybody feels lonely at times is some help, but not much, and your inability to find the right or true source or cause of your loneliness is as painful as is the loneliness itself.

We think back through our lives, thinking that loneliness didn't hit at all when we were young, except — oh, yes — in certain, rare, specific situations: mom in the hospital, siblings gone somewhere without you, being sent off to the relatives while your parents holiday, starting a new school — that kind of thing. Or later, in adulthood, betrayal, divorce, living alone, changing cities, children leaving home, without the money to do whatever it is you want to do, dreaming of some life you can never have. Now, in old age, though, our loneliness baffles us no matter what we do to alleviate it; we resent it and start searching through the past to try to discover how we have come to this state.

Judith Shulevitz, writing in *The New Republic* in 2013, tells us:

And yet loneliness is made as well as given, and at a very early age. Deprive us of the attention of a loving, reliable parent, and, if nothing happens to make up for that lack, we'll tend toward loneliness for the rest of our lives. Not only that, but our loneliness will probably make us moody, self-doubting, angry, pessimistic, shy, and hypersensitive to criticism. Recently, it has become clear that some of these problems reflect how our brains are shaped from our first moments of life.

When I read this passage, just now, at nearly eighty years of age, I froze, so accurate a description it was of how I gradually, over my adulthood, have come to see myself. To this day I fight those tendencies so I can live a more normal life; that is, so I don't die of self-imposed loneliness. And still, I catch myself dodging out of an event as soon as it ends, just when everybody else is gathering to network, bond, secure alliances, gossip, chat, and just socialize enjoyably for half an hour before, feeling satisfied, they turn toward home. Or else I refuse a social invitation because it intimidates me too much, even though everybody else will be having a good time, and I probably would, too, if I could just muster the courage to initiate conversations, and if I didn't think that the slightest, most fleeting expression means the person I'm talking to is bored by me, or has taken a dislike to me. That I have, once again, said something immeasurably stupid, or offensive — or have made an enemy when I was trying to make a friend. Rather than suffer through that again, I tell myself, *I would rather be alone.*

Not all the roots of loneliness arise from childhood experience. When I first became aware of myself as old, and when both my parents (and all the older relatives) had died, as well as two of my four sisters and my husband (the other two sisters, my son, and his family live far away), leaving me pretty much permanently alone in a physical sense, I began to feel like the last member of my tribe left on earth. For the first time, I understood in the deepest part of my being what the true loneliness of orphans, and of those who define themselves or are so defined by society as Other, as not belonging, really is. I began to understand why the elderly are too often lonely people.

But this kind of loneliness is attached to being in the flesh, to once being firmly related to others, once a member of a large family with many members nearby. The soul remains connected to the dead, as if they were all still alive, but the body is bereft, and the mind rests in a kind of melancholy, awed confusion, and dismay. More than once I have heard old people say, in a puzzled, sad way, something like, "I have outlived my life." I have said it myself. How can it be that I remain alive and on earth when the significant people of the life I have lived are now only ghosts? I have overstayed my life; my still being alive is surely a mistake; I was meant to go when they did.

When I consider my own loneliness, now, in my old age, as I have done both on purpose and inadvertently, I count my blessings: a nice home, enough money to pay my bills, pretty good health for my age, a few good old friends in other provinces I can talk to on the phone, a few new friends with whom to visit and go to movies and plays, a brain that, though not as good as it used to be, is still working well enough. These thoughts cure me for the moment, but let my guard down, and there it is again, like a mangy grey coyote that shadows me everywhere I go, and lies, forgotten by me, at my feet under the table when I'm lunching with a friend at home. Nonetheless, I know that the moment the door latch clicks behind her, that coyote will crawl out from under the table and rub against my leg once more. And I am baffled by it, too, and thoroughly annoyed with myself, because I knew — I know — better, if only I could remember what I know.

I was lonely because I had no significant other reading the newspaper in the other room. But as I adjusted to my single state, stifling that yearning, I turned to the philosophers for instruction on the good life, the happy life, and in reading them, I suddenly remembered a teaching from many years ago, when I was wandering alone on the prairie one day, immensely sad, full of self-pity, and trying to understand where my dismal feelings came from.

There really was no one thing that I could pinpoint: I was sad because I was alive and did not have every single thing I had ever wanted, did not even know all the things I wanted, and I believe now that it was the latter that made me saddest. I was alive and I was a human being, and wanting is the condition of being human. Words appeared in my head, or perhaps it was what I have called the "voiceless voice" that spoke to me. *This too is illusion*, it said, and, at once, it straightened my head right around. Good God, I thought. How could I have forgotten that? Wisdom might sometimes come in such a flash, but

I have learned you have to stick with it, or it will leave you as clueless as you were before it hit.

Loneliness isn't a social construct in itself, although social conditions can certainly create it: the loneliness of the prisoner, the loneliness of those doomed to live a life that they think is not the one they would have chosen for themselves, the loneliness of the elderly caused by ageism. To suffer from loneliness is part of the human condition and must always have existed.

But it hasn't always been named as such. Shakespeare (1564–1616), our greatest expert on everything human, left behind no indelible quotations about loneliness, although he did about every other human experience. He is credited with coining the word "lonely" in *Coriolanus* (written between 1605 and 1608), in which his protagonist says "though I go alone, like to a lonely dragon . . ." (IV, i, 30). But the word then meant "solitary, lone; unfrequented." For Shakespeare, was loneliness fully tied to the condition of being unhappily in love? Or else did it concern the supposed loneliness of the dead — a state typically depicted then as being terrifyingly alone? Nonetheless, his tragic heroes certainly suffered from what we would today simply call loneliness. King Lear, Hamlet, Timon of Athens, Coriolanus, Titus Andronicus in their extremes of rage, grief, and humiliation were also lonely people.

The word "loneliness," according to the OED, was first used by Sir Philip Sidney, in *Arcadia*, in 1586, the same year he died, and when Shakespeare would have been twenty-two, and not yet churning out masterworks. The quotation I cite at the beginning of this essay, from Milton, is recognized as the earliest major quotation about loneliness, and is dated

1645, twenty-nine years after Shakespeare's death. And yet "lonely" didn't take on its contemporary meaning, "dejected for want of company," according to both the Online Etymology Dictionary and the OED (which is perhaps more reliable), until 1811 when Byron wrote in his poem "One Struggle More": "Though pleasure fires the maddening soul, / The heart — the heart is lonely still!" Which, I confess, makes me think of people who "swing" and take part in group sex. I'm willing to bet their hearts are lonely still. Still, I am inclined to think we have entered the impenetrable territory of the different mindsets of people of different eras. I leave further pondering as to whether we are talking about etymology and naming, or psychology, philosophy, or sociology, to the experts.

Of our era, though, Thomas Dumm wrote, in his 2008 book *Loneliness as a Way of Life*, that the "very texture of modern life is inflected by loneliness." He continues:

It is a leading experience through which we shape our perceptions of the world. It informs our deepest longings and aversions, an element infiltrating every part of our existence. Loneliness thus may be thought of as being a profoundly political experience because it is instrumental in the shaping and exercise of power, the meaning of individuality, and the ways in which justice is to be comprehended and realized in the world.

Today, loneliness is so ubiquitous an experience that in January 2018, the British government created a Ministry of Loneliness and gave it to a young female minister responsible for several other portfolios as well, leaving me to wonder how much they meant to garner a high "cuteness" score, and how seriously they took this initiative. In Canada, at least, governments at all levels are beginning to set up bodies to study the condition, usually those aspects with measurable parameters, and to devise ways of alleviating it where they find it, although this is chiefly (I think), although not exclusively, among senior citizens.

But the disabled are surely another population afflicted by loneliness, as are all those who exist on the edges of our contemporary society: those with skin colour differing from that of the majority, those whose command of English is less than perfect because they grew up speaking one or more other languages, those suffering from mental illness. In 2018, a British study found that young people suffer from loneliness more than any other group.

But for most of us, the fundamental condition of loneliness will remain, even if at a diminished level, and it will ebb and flow throughout our lives. But psychoanalyst James Hollis writes:

> We are all lonely, even when amid crowds and
> in committed relationships. When we are alone,
> we are still with someone; we are with ourselves.
> The question is how are we with ourselves?
> Those who manage to find respect for themselves,
> who learn to dialogue with themselves, who find
> that their dreams and other such phenomena
> are communicating with them from some deeper
> place within them are not really alone.

Hollis offers a psychoanalytic solution, deeply learned and intensely felt, and one that most people would be grateful for (and content with), but I think that although helpful, Hollis's response is still not quite the full answer to the problem of loneliness. Remember that we are all afraid, even the greatest heroes and heroines among us. My own feeling is that perhaps that empty spot that nonetheless pains us so deeply is yearning for what we have lost — our mother, perhaps, a spouse, or a child, the original home, the way of life we left behind. Thomas Dumm delves into this, and writes,

Our loneliness is always deepest in those moments when we face the terror of nothing. But nothing rarely appears as itself; instead, it takes on many guises, most of which connect back to the ultimate nothing, death, or non-existence, that blank page.

And how do we deal with that? Of course, I think of myself as a person with a long history of being stifled by my own fears; and now, in old age, I think of the foolish ones: to drive in heavy traffic, to go to places where I know no one, to go out at night — all fears that beset the elderly. I have wondered about them, berated myself over them, tried to overcome them, but I think I see now that although there are legitimate things for old people to fear, I suspect they are ultimately related to approaching nothingness, "that blank page" Dumm writes of.

One of the things that most puzzled me during the more than thirty years I spent in rural solitude was that even as I was often brought to an absolute physical halt by the beauty I saw, I was at the same time stricken painfully in the heart by the sight. Looking closer, I identified it as yearning, and then, of course, I asked, yearning for what? In the end, I gave the yearning the name of loneliness.

If I were more religious than I am, I might say that the feeling was yearning for the place we come from before we are born. But I don't quite believe that, although I would like to. Is it about the human search for perfection, the perfection we find only in great works of art and out in the landscape (as I have called being in nature in my books)? I think that we yearn for perfect peace, which doesn't mean being in perfect solitude, or comatose, or brain-dead, but for peace in the heart — a peaceful heart in the midst of the multitudes and the tumult, chaos, violence, sorrow, and beauty of everyday life. And that, we can never have, but in the work of art or the sunset, we perhaps have intimations of that perfect peace, and that is why we feel a certain sadness.

I have at times forgotten all about loneliness, and, if asked, would have said, "What? Me? What are you talking about?" and wouldn't even have been able to remember what the condition felt like. It's hard to be lonely when in the midst of sex; the act rather occupies you fully, at least for a few minutes. And I wasn't lonely giving birth, although I was frightened, in pain, and perhaps indignant that this was bloody well asking too much of me. Or when I held my dearest preschooler tightly in my arms. Moments, flashes, the occasional long afternoon in the countryside, when dreaming, when lost in my work, the in-the-zone state that athletes and performers talk about, when struggling to understand an idea, whenever I have been focused on something. Nor was I lonely when I was walking on the prairie alone, and my consciousness moved out beyond its normal limits and allowed me a larger sense of the world.

It took nearly eighty years of living through happy things and sad things and through many of the torments that beset humanity before I began to see how right the philosophers were (living their own torments, I'm sure), that we are creatures of desire, creatures of the imagination, that to subdue such natural and vital processes takes a lifetime of repeated experience and the work that follows. No wonder wisdom suggests that we learn to focus on the now, forget the past, and stop worrying about the future. Only then does the sorrow vanish, only then do we erase loneliness.

But how would my life have changed if my young teacher had come looking for me, and, speaking to me encouragingly, had brought me to the others and ensured that I found a place in the game? Maybe I was waiting for her to do that, although I remember soon realizing that nobody would, one of the first revelations of my life. That I was all alone, not by choice, because I wanted to be with the other kids, but I wanted something else, too. Or maybe my proclivity for solitude was entrenched even before I even attended school. Perhaps my need for solitude, despite its sometime companion loneliness, had been instilled in my soul at conception, and it would be up to me, as I grew, to find a balance where I could. But if my teacher had rescued me from my desire for solitude, and my self-willed loneliness, would I be a writer today?

COLD ANKLES

When I got up one morning a couple of weeks ago and wandered from my bedroom into the main area of my condo — kitchen, living room, dining room — to make coffee, I smelled gas. Odd, because my home runs on electricity, although I do have a gas fireplace, but I could see at the other end of the room that the fireplace's switch was in the Off position, and when I walked closer to it, I could see that its pilot light was burning cheerily away, and I could not smell gas coming from it. Puzzled, but hardly concerned, I went from the still faintly gas-smelling kitchen area back into my bedroom, where I couldn't detect any unnatural scent, then back into the main room, where I found that the gas odour I'd smelled only minutes before had vanished. I thought I must have imagined it. As I would later say to the gas company man, who stared at me as if at a lunatic, "I'm seventy-eight years old: I don't hear very well, my eyesight is going, flavours don't taste like they used to, so why shouldn't my sense of smell be faulty, too?"

I don't remember much about my first sixty-five or so years beyond the usual markers: graduations, marriages, childbirths, deaths, and moves from here to there. I *could* remember, but two or three years ago, after I had finished my life-survey that old people seem to need to do, I decided against even thinking about my past, except inadvertently, when I would stop myself at once. I had begun to see the incidents, the conversations, the emotions of the long flow of my life as in themselves without meaning, and had begun to suspect that the real meaning of my life was something else entirely, although what that was, I didn't know. But I had also kept journals from when I was about forty until about seventy-three. Every day, I had written in them what I thought and felt about people in my life, or ideas I was musing on, or happenings I had played a part in, as well as recording some of my dreams — those that were more vivid and seemingly significant than others.

When I finally felt I'd finished with my inadvertent, yet somehow inevitable, mental life-review, I found myself curious about the journals, and went back to look through them. I think that, for most of the years I wrote in them, I must have held at the back of my mind the notion that I was writing important things about who I was, that one day would show me as insightful, even brilliant, a person to be reckoned with. Now, I suppose not surprisingly, I found their very continued existence revealed only my narcissism, and that their contents were repetitious as well as banal, and, too often, simply trivial.

Worse, they revealed the size of my secret ambition, too much about my shame at my failures, humiliations, and mistakes, as well as a lot of other things that I never wanted anybody — ever, anywhere — to know about.

The journals so embarrassed me that I decided to burn them all while I still could, the elderly person on her own being all too well aware that at any moment the Great Catastrophe can strike. But my gas fireplace, although it does give off heat, is mostly ornamental, and is sealed with a thick sheet of heat-tempered glass. Besides, over the ten days since that morning I first smelled the gas, I had smelled it, though faintly, on several more occasions. Each time, the odour vanished almost as fast as I noticed it, and the pilot light was still burning steadily, but I was, nonetheless, nervous about turning on my fireplace. A friend with an old-fashioned wood-burning fireplace said that I should use it to burn the journals, that she and her husband would be out in the afternoons for the next couple of days, and, thus, that I "could have a little ceremony," before or during the burning. I smiled and thanked her, while privately thinking that would be the day I'd be so sentimental, or so hopeful, or could bring myself to believe the journals were of any importance at all in the larger scheme of things. I just wanted to get rid of them before I kicked the bucket and my son read them, or worse. I thought of Sylvia Plath and her *published* journals, a fate too horrible to contemplate, not that, I kept reminding myself, anybody would want to publish mine.

I wanted to get the job done as fast as possible, but I was, of course, also concerned about not burning down my friend's house. I found what we used to call when I was an art student an x-Acto knife — I've no idea what they are called now — to use on the journals, because otherwise they would have taken far too long to burn. So, I sliced off the cardboard covers at the bindings and tossed them one by one behind me as I knelt in front of the fireplace. I was immensely pleased with myself. Easy-peasy, I was thinking, having expected burning the journals to be ever so much harder, maybe even impossible.

As I began to tear the closely written pages from their bindings and throw them into the fire, I stopped to read some of the dreams I'd logged, as the only subject in the journals that didn't now fill me with annoyance, boredom, or even, sometimes, disgust. Over my adult life I have had a few dreams that turned out to be not merely garbled reality, nor clever statements about the condition of my psyche then, but that, in time, turned out to be prescient. I don't think I'm special in this; I think everybody has such dreams, but since the arrival of our overruling belief in the god Science, cannot allow ourselves to notice them, or if we do notice them, we dismiss them out of hand. If any of us wonders about such dreams at all, we wonder privately.

In my burning that first afternoon, I came across a dream I had about five years earlier, about a man I had known for forty years, and with whom, after the breakdown of our first marriages, and then after our second spouses both died (his first, then mine), I had had brief liaisons, both times going nowhere, although we always remained close friends. In the dream, he was trying to persuade a woman I didn't know to go to bed with him, and was being rebuffed. He was wearing only trousers, and most startling was that his skin was paperwhite, this because, the dream said, he had cancer. In real

34

life, he was a strong, healthy man in his late sixties, his skin darkened by his vigorous outdoor life. Women, as far as I knew, lit up when they saw him; they didn't refuse him. But because it had been so vivid, I had written down the dream — see what I mean about trivia? — even though it made almost no sense to me.

When I woke from the dream, though, I remembered that some years earlier, one morning as I was about to mount the post office steps, I had passed a middle-aged woman I knew only slightly coming down them. Her face had been that same unnatural paper-white as my friend's body was in my dream. I remembered my involuntary chill, shock even, when I saw her strange too-white face, and how I brushed off what I'd seen, deciding that her extreme pallor must be due to sickness, although I didn't know any details about her life. But a few days later, she and four of her relatives were killed in a horrific car crash, as they drove, idiotically, through a particularly bad blizzard. Slowly, over the intervening years — no, I must have known it at once, but wouldn't admit it as far too strange — I had come to admit the woman's too-white face as notice of her impending death, that, somehow, I had *seen*. So, of course I immediately recognized that the dream about my dear old friend must be saying the same thing about him.

I simply refused to believe it, though; it seemed ridiculous, and although I recorded the dream, I forgot about it until I noticed it as I tossed journal pages into the fire. For the first time, I saw that the dream had come roughly three years before his diagnosis and four before his death from cancer. Maybe even at the time, cancer had started brewing in his body, long before there were symptoms or it was detectable

by ordinary means. Personally, in my old age, I have come to
think that most knowledge is available to us, but we all determinedly keep the channels blocked. We do not want to know.
How would we live if we knew?

Kneeling in front of the fireplace, surrounded by
collapsed journal covers and piles of worthless pages
crammed with writing recording years of my life, I thought
of how my old friend and I had loved each other since not
long after our first meeting, when we were both married
to other people; how we loved each other on through our
second marriages, both our spouses eventually dying, and
then into our widower- and widowhood, when we were free
to be together. And yet, although for a while we turned to
each other in our bereavement, we did not become a couple,
as most people would have predicted, me included. I have
a lot of ideas about why that didn't happen, but perhaps he
saw, as I eventually began to, that our lives were now too
different — our love was both deeper and no longer entirely
romantic in nature — that it was too late for us, if, indeed, the
right time would ever present itself. Hadn't history shown, I
began to think, that there would be no right time? How very
odd that seems to me now, and I wonder if Shakespeare knew
something more about "star-crossed lovers," as he seems to
have done about so many human things, than we are able to
discern from his play.

Instead, after a while, he began to date younger women.
I couldn't blame him, even felt tender toward him, knowing
that he was no longer alone, solitude slowly killing his
warmth and generosity. And I felt mature enough to deal
with his turning away from me, or perhaps I thought he would

eventually come back. At his funeral, though, I found out that he had been in a relationship with a much younger woman, that she had been living in his house with him, I had no idea for how long; I didn't even know her name. And yet, when we talked, he would refer to the man I was seeing as "that guy," in a disgruntled way that always made me secretly smile.

He had been dead about eighteen months when I began occasionally to smell gas in my condo. Ever since my husband's death, whenever I had a household problem — mechanical, electrical, sometimes even legal — I would phone him, and his voice would at once grow strong, his tone authoritative, as he explained what I needed to do. But he was dead, and as I now lived in an all-female world, I knew no one else I could call for easy, good advice. As the gas smell came, lingered a few moments, and then dissipated, I must have been hoping it would just go away without my having to do anything.

Once I got over being angry at what I saw as his betrayal in not telling me about his new partner, I thought that he had not been truthful because he hadn't wanted to lose my friendship — our long phone calls, the way we helped each other, he relying on my women's knowledge, mostly about his children, and I on his men's, mostly about household machinery and equipment, what to do about things that broke down. Only recently it came to me that the woman in the dream I couldn't see clearly and didn't recognize, who rejected him, might have been me. I remembered how he had looked so troubled as he gazed at me the last time we saw each other, and in his last message, for the only time in all our years of knowing each other, had addressed me as "dearest." Instead of burning that page, I put it aside, and it still sits on my desk.

Even though I smelled gas a number of times, I stubbornly refused to call the fire department, or the gas company, or even to bring in a neighbour to see if she could smell it too; I didn't even allow myself to think seriously about doing such things. I knew all along, though, that my stubbornness was bizarre, and, in an incoherent way, I believe I knew why I refused to do the sensible thing. Perhaps the gas smell would go away for good. Or not. In which case — well, I never looked at the inevitable explosion and my own death straight in the eye. I was, I see now, toying with death. Gambling? Hoping?

Like most people, I've had lots of reasons over the years to contemplate suicide, and never went any further, although when feeling my worst, I couldn't stop thinking about it. Once, I even made myself laugh out loud when I realized that every single thing I looked at, from the shallow stream behind the house to the kitchen carving knife, the bottle of sleeping pills, my basket of embroidery thread, the pillow on my bed, and even the lemon tarts on the counter, I saw as potential tools. Not when my first husband left me and I might have had a nervous breakdown, not when at my master's degree comprehensive I froze and couldn't answer questions I'd known the answers to five minutes before, and not when two of my siblings died too young. Not even when my husband died suddenly, and left me alone, and with a large business to clean up and dispose of. A normal life. Pure hell, in other words. So why didn't I just strike a match when I smelled the gas?

I am glad my nuttiness didn't kill my neighbours — not the one on oxygen, nor the mysteriously jovial couple who keep such odd hours, nor even the strange person, with whom, even as we deliver Christmas greetings and cookies to each other, I am uneasy. They didn't deserve to die because I was toying with death. Maybe that was all fate had in mind: I was being tested. Would I strike a match? Or would I call the fire department? I chose to do neither; I was determined that fate should do its job and decide for itself. Anyway, I wasn't in the total misery of the usual suicide; I was merely the old person devoid of all, or nearly all, illusions and, just possibly, beginning to understand what death is, and what it is for.

Eventually, workers repairing the exterior of our building smelled the gas and knocked on my door. I had forgotten that I had an outside gas valve for a barbecue, because, not owning a barbecue, I had never used the connection. The workmen said that they had found the valve open, and that whether I smelled gas or not probably depended on which way the wind happened to be blowing. But even with the valve closed, the gas smell steadily increased. Puzzled, we called our building's mechanical service company. The emergency man arrived quickly, called the gas server company at once, and began to move an electronic device carefully over my wall, searching out the source of the leak, while conferring in a hushed voice with his boss on a phone he held tucked between his shoulder and ear. I should have been afraid then, but I wasn't. The gas expert arrived and took charge, telling the clueless condo management company representative over the phone, "Lady, *I'm* the guy the fire department calls!"

By then, my tiny kitchen area was full of men — the contractor, the condo board rep, the mechanical-server-company man, the gas company rep — all of us waiting and watching, speaking softly if at all, and none of us scurried away or even acted afraid. Then the emergency worker discovered that a carpenter repairing my outside wall had pounded a nail directly into my gas line. Two of the men left immediately, muttering softly to each other, for the mechanical room to turn off the gas. Later, as I pecked away at my computer in the next room, I heard the two men who were tearing out the plasterboard in my kitchen to reach the leaky line in order to repair it, talking. "This wall must have been full of gas," one said. "Yeah, scary," the other said. Even then I was not retroactively afraid, and went back to typing merrily away.

Maybe I didn't do anything about the smell because, having done my life-review, I am pretty much past ire over the events of my life, I recognize the foolishness of my desires and aspirations — although I still wonder in a puzzled way over every one of them — and, despite having owned up to my ugly acts and my cruelties, accept that there is no way on earth to be free of them. Like Leonard Cohen is supposed to have been the evening of his dying, even to the point of dancing and singing as he waited (which turns out to be emphatically not true — why do true believers so often turn out to be liars?) — I, too, would be relieved, even happy, to say goodbye to this earthly life. Or so I tell myself.

I once, briefly, knew an ex-priest who had spent his adult life in the farthest reaches of southeast Asia among the "hill people," as he said, who told me that when they were cursed by others, they would go into their huts, "turn their faces to the wall and die," and when after a fraught moment, I asked, "But how do they die?" he answered irritably, as if I should have known, "They let their spirits go."

I hadn't the courage yet to turn my face to the wall, and I wasn't ready: I wanted to see my child one more time;

I wanted to finish the book I was working on. But, at the same time, I wondered if my paralysis was only simple denial, not wanting to take responsibility, not wanting to have to deal with the racket and the workmen and whatever construction would follow as more nuisance than I'm able to bear anymore, and not the product of some admirable, elevated wisdom. Maybe I am only suffering from grandiosity and delusion, from madness, and should have done the normal thing and called the fire department at once.

But if my very real gas leak was a test from beyond, I failed it, and have been kidding myself about my readiness for death all along. Last night I caught myself thinking I should buy some new socks, as winter is approaching, and my ankles are already cold.

The first afternoon I spent burning my journals went slowly. I was careful about cutting off the covers just so, and setting them aside. Cautiously, in order not to get too hot a fire, I burned only a couple of pages at a time. I didn't want to heat my friend's house too much, or, worse, to set it on fire. But on the second afternoon, although somewhere, distantly, I still thought how I must be careful, I lost myself in the burning. Page after page I threw in the fire; I tore the books apart and began to throw in clusters of pages; I did not notice anymore where I was or remember what reason I had for burning the journals, or wonder whether I was making a mistake, deliberately destroying something that had been so important in my life, that was, in fact, a deeply intimate record of the more than thirty years of my life, my mid-life, when I had lived on a ranch and had been a rancher's wife, had learned to ride a horse and to chase cows and to watch the sky with a wrinkled brow and to count the millimetres of rain — me, an academic and eventually a much-published writer. I burned, ripped, threw, burned more. I wasn't angry, I wasn't exactly sad either. My actions were, at least partly, mechanical, but as I ripped and tore, threw and burned, I moved out of myself somehow, in some way I can't explain: a renunciation? an acceptance? Of what? Of a third of my life that had permanently ended, both the good and the bad that, feeling I had no choice, I had left behind forever. It was, too, an acknowledgement that I was real, that my life had been real, that it was, indeed and irrevocably, done.

Only as I fed the last pages into the fire, the flames rearing up orange, red, blue, and I watched them crumble, then blacken, and disappear into ash, the fire dying back down again, and finally going out, me leaning back on my knees from where I had been bent over the fire for — how long? I did not know — I realized that I knelt within a cocoon of warmth of a different quality than the crackling, searing natural heat from my fire. I saw that even though I hadn't willed it or meant it, and don't believe in such things anymore, the burning of my journals had become by its very nature a ritual act. And I can't tell you, even now, if burning my journals was a good or a bad thing to have done. If burning my journals changed anything, about the life they recorded or my life to come.

STORAGE

On October 31, 2013, six years after my rancher husband's death and five after my move to Calgary, I finally emptied my five-by-fifteen-foot storage locker in Swift Current. The locker held mostly books — boxes and boxes of them — along with several boxes containing household items that ranked high on the list of things I'm unlikely to use again: table-cloths and matching napkins and odd items such as the nineteenth-century perfume bottle that had belonged to my Scottish grandmother and had come to her from a relative of her stepmother, who had once been a "companion" to great ladies, or, at least, to wealthy women. More boxes contained records, which the tax department required I keep and lug around for more years. Plus pictures — some framed paintings, some framed photographs — that I didn't really want anymore but couldn't throw away, and also couldn't find room to hang in my new big-city condo.

I had been emptying the locker for the five years I'd lived in Calgary. I was by this time driving a new, small car with a tiny area for carrying items, but I couldn't simply hire a truck and move everything at once, because in Calgary I had no place to put any of it (except perhaps the pink and gold perfume bottle), and I was reluctant to move the stuff to a storage locker in Calgary, where lockers cost five times what they cost in Swift Current. I supposed if everything in the locker went up in flames, I wouldn't miss any of it, unless, of course, Revenue Canada started demanding documents that had turned to ashes. So, year after year, odd trip after odd trip, I carted three or five boxes back to my condo, emptied them bit by bit, giving away some things, integrating others into my new life, and throwing away — with tremendous difficulty — a part of each load. Finally, after about four years, the locker's contents were down to nothing but books. After one trip, I managed to find by sheer luck two book sales at the same time, and got rid of six boxes that way.

I never wanted to lose a single book from the approximately three thousand I had owned, but I had come to face that some were precious to me, and some, out of a mixture of vanity and curiosity, I merely liked owning. They were the ones that had to go. I was even reduced near the end to throwing away paperback novels. They weren't in perfect condition, nor new novels by a long shot, and most of them could be had anywhere; there was nothing precious about them. I did it when nobody was looking, feeling like a philistine, or like the beleaguered librarians trying to make room in the library in the digital age, and nobody — but nobody — understanding how they could throw out thousands of books *just because in fifty years nobody had checked them out*. What had that to do with anything? The library of Alexandria came to mind, destroyed by the barbarians, all that most ancient knowledge lost forever, and the digital age, those fragile pieces of celluloid and then of apparently nothing at all: gigabytes of nothingness. Preservable through the ages? I doubted it.

But this dispersal was the dying of a dream of myself as an intellectual: this is what the books had represented to me, and I always knew they had; my pride in them was based on that self-image. I cherished the books because their ragged and usually dusty rows in a room full of bookshelves said to me and to others what I didn't dare to say out loud: I am not just another ignorant country woman with a mind dulled by too many children, too many years driving the baler or the combine, chasing cows on horseback or with a truck, making too many pickles and Halloween costumes, watching too many peewee hockey games, running too many bake sales or cooking too many fowl supper turkeys. I am a mind.

I *had* to be brave; I had no alternative. I discovered, as I took the last five boxes of books to the regional library, and stored yet another box of papers in my car to take back to Calgary (where I would have no room for it), as I drove across town to the owners of the storage units to return the key and get back my deposit, that I would not be able so easily to empty my mind of my storage locker. Instead of the elation I'd expected, that weight-off-the-shoulders feeling, relief simply did not come. I felt instead a mixture of small pleasure that I would not have to make such a trip again, that

I had tied up one of the last of the ends severed by Peter's death, and an uneasy sadness that, short of the regular trips to my husband's grave, I'd seen the last of the countryside where I'd lived for so long and now seemed to want nothing as much as to escape from there forever. But for all the years I'd wanted with something close to desperation to be rid of that storage locker, the contents evaporated, the burden it represented put down, I wondered why I was not elated. I had expected to be elated, had planned to be, so why could I not muster one shout of joy? Even stranger was the feeling that I could not believe I had emptied it. I couldn't figure out why, in the place in my mind, or heart, or soul where I stored tasks, duty, responsibility, and encumbrances, the contents of the storage locker were still there, filled to overflowing, impossibly burdensome still.

I couldn't dismiss my past, although I urgently wanted to. On the highway heading back to Calgary, I thought of how I had come to terms with the loss of my childhood as everyone does eventually, even though some people go back to it in old age. Mine was certainly interesting, but on the whole, not really that great to live in; I could view it as I might view a movie, wonderful colour — rich greens, crimson-tinted shadows — and unexplained movement, lots of passion, sorrow and shame, but in some very real way, though I viewed it with a distant warmth and sometimes an equally distant pity, I now felt my childhood was disconnected from the grown-up me. That was just fine. Nobody lives that pioneer life anymore, or that small-town life of rafting on sloughs on the edge of town, of racing through poplar forests, stick in hand, screaming for no particular reason, skating wherever there was a patch of ice until your feet were so cold you could hardly get your skates off to walk home. No, my childhood was a visceral dream that I could visit if I wanted to, but mostly I didn't want to.

I had put my adolescence and teenagerhood behind me, too, partly because I had written about them in a book, *The Girl in Saskatoon: A Meditation on Friendship, Memory, and Murder.* With both parents dead, the people I knew from those days for the most part were gone, living lives unknown to me, and I felt I had absorbed that person into my larger self, not without sadness, not without shame and sometimes a kind of woebegone pride; that *was* me; no need to revisit it. I had come to the resolution that I would never rid myself of my long first marriage, which had produced my only child, my beloved son, now a man of fifty years, but I tried never to think about it; my second marriage, more than double the length of the first, and with its terrible ending, I was just beginning to emerge from. The storage locker held my past, it represented what I had lost; shedding it finally should have meant I had finished with that past, reconciled with it, and should have at last freed me for my future. Yet my joy, which I was trying to sink into as I raced down the highway, was bemused and incomplete, laced with emotion at which I didn't dare look too closely, knowing all too well already of what it was composed.

Where I had often, by rising very early, made the five-hour trip to Saskatoon from the hay farm in southwestern Saskatchewan and back again in time to cook a late dinner, and didn't find ten hours too daunting, I now was completely worn out by a mere six-hour drive in excellent weather and with perfect roads from Calgary to Swift Current. Not just worn out, but left with thighs that ached as though I'd run a marathon, my always-fragile left shoulder — a childhood injury compounded by an adult one — too painful to move, and my wrist and forearm aching steadily from what I suppose must be another arthritic intrusion. I knew I had made my last six-hour drive in one day — barring, of course, racing ahead of a flood, typhoon, or invading army.

I had begun to feel old. I'd already been old, depending on how one chooses to count, and I'm going to start at sixty, for thirteen years. I had never felt old before though; that was the difference. Every senior citizen can name the year when he or she actually began to feel old, can sometimes even name the moment when the truth struck home at last: in the middle of a golf game, after a surgery, or an illness, or a fall, or unexpected heartbreak — death, departure, retirement. Or even just walking down a street and, without noticing, avoiding stepping up onto the curb as too much effort, and suddenly realizing you've been avoiding stepping onto curbs for some time. When I got out of the car, it took me a minute to creak upright.

Days later, I continued to feel as though I carried the burden of that storage locker and its contents on my shoulders. I have had throughout my adult life (or so I've always believed) a capacity to put things behind me when I am done with them, to wash my hands of them, to walk away as if they had never happened or existed. This ability or desire was part of what kept propelling me forward in life, and although I wasn't exactly proud of being able to do it, I refused to examine it; I had a mental picture of myself striding away, back straight, chin up, into the future. But the storage locker, I continued to drag behind, as the penitent played by Jeremy Irons in *The Mission* drags up and down mountains his load of iron vessels and objects connected to the church, an image I will never be able to forget. In the film, someone eventually takes pity on him, walks over, and with a knife cuts the rope that attaches the load, freeing him. I guessed nobody would free me from the storage locker. I would have to do that myself, and *how* I would became a subject that I continued to mull over, day after day.

A few days later, still recovering from the twelve-hour trip made over two days, as I lay on the sofa reading, something went funny in my head. I thought that maybe I was having a stroke: I blinked, I looked around, I counted to twenty mentally to make sure I still could, I sat up, puzzled, and everything was exactly as it had been before that moment, both inside and outside. Not a stroke, then. It had been on the left side, deep inside, my mind's eye had seen the dark red shading to blackness of the body's interior, but nothing was moving, no blood was flowing; there had been a sort of sudden muted buzzing, a break in the middle of whatever it was, a milder repeat, and then, everything went back to normal.

I am still puzzling over it, but within a few hours, reading something else, although I've forgotten what exactly — somebody's discussion of aging — I suddenly realized that I had fourteen years left of life at the very least, barring the usual catastrophes, but one doesn't plan for catastrophes; one plans for normal life. Therefore, I would live at least another fourteen years. I would then be only eighty-seven, the normal life expectancy for a North American female already of a certain age. I had made this assertion after Peter's death, when I told myself I had twenty years left, and each year since, I had knocked off one, until I was now at fourteen. And yet, despite thinking that in a perfectly rational way, even having said to friends, "fourteen years is lots of time in which to do things," and smiling smugly, I had not really understood a word I was saying. That afternoon, lying on the sofa, my brain underwent a major shift, and for the first time, the truth I had been mouthing became real. Everything around me grew clearer, brighter, developed the sharp edges and outlines of real, solid life. I saw how I had begun to drift, begun to give up things (even while telling aged friends that old age was not about giving up but about gaining — sententious fool that I was). I threw off the afghan, swung around, put my feet on the floor, looked around, and considered what this shift meant.

When I was in high school, I had a plan for my life: I would go to university, I would get at least one degree if not more, I would then go on to a profession, and I would join the middle class. It wasn't much, but it was a plan. I would marry, apparently I would have children, I would rise in my profession, I would buy a house and a car, and so on. Now, finally, I had come to the inevitable realization that I needed a plan for my fourteen remaining years. I would have been ashamed of myself for behaving as if I were living in a dream that would soon end, so that I didn't have to keep on with my studies, or work hard at my writing, or my reading, or travel if it felt like too much effort (and it certainly did), or put myself out in any way if I didn't feel like it. But in the face of my approaching end, everything seemed futile. This was not despair; it was not depression; I was having a good, interesting life, if a non-goal-oriented one. Besides, I told myself, hadn't I been an extremely hard-working woman all my life? Wasn't it time I got a rest, time I just floated around and did what I felt like doing without having to look after anybody else, or meet even my own expectations for myself? Even the closing of the storage locker constantly nagged at me, and I had to remind myself that I had emptied it.

And so, at this critical passage in my life, I came to some conclusion about, or accommodation with, my past, and I understood that I had to turn my face to my future. But age was demanding a new effort from me, something different. I could not rid myself of my past, and I was learning that no matter how I finessed those memories, they would come back to strike me in the middle of the night, when they would wake me, and then I wouldn't sleep again no matter how hard I tried to shove them back below consciousness. Or they would strike me as I crossed a room, and I would slow, and tears might suddenly form in my eyes so that I had to wipe them away, even as I called myself a fool and expelled air through my nose in exasperation at myself. This occurrence, however, was not omnipresent, not daily or nightly; those dream-memories mostly had faded, but I was coming to know and slowly to accept that this storage locker would, in my life, never be emptied.

I lived now in Calgary; I was perched there. As I tried to conceive of a meaningful future as much as I had led a meaningful past, I focused, of course, on myself as an artist, a writer. If I had another self, I did not know what it was; I didn't think I had another self; I didn't want another self.

And so I tried to go back to my writing life — I had never stopped writing — but my writing life refused to return, by which I mean the hours of absolute concentration on whatever work I was doing, the afternoon hours I devoted to serious reading, the way I woke early in the morning and went straight to my desk.

Finally, a couple of years into my Calgary sojourn, for so I still thought of it, not as *my life*, but some sort of an interlude before — what? I did not know what; I didn't examine it — I signed a contract to write a new book. This was, I thought, exactly what I needed to turn me back into a real writer, instead of a mere scribbler playing at writing, imitating the real writer I had been before my husband's death and all that so relentlessly and implacably followed it. I would be single-minded again; I would be obsessed; now my life would once again smooth itself out like a river, its steady flow disturbed by nothing but the most catastrophic events.

Instead, I struggled for a week, or two weeks, perhaps even longer, to mentally (or was it spiritually?) *conceive* of this book. I had written a proposal for it, of course, plus a fairly detailed outline, and the next step, that first page or first paragraph or even first sentence should have been easy. But I couldn't seem to get started. I backed off and sharpened metaphoric pencils, washed the kitchen floor instead, went out for a walk when the temperature was just right, came back to stare at my computer, and then turned on the television. Finally, I knew I had to stop all this avoidance. I had a contract after all, I had to write, and to do that I had to figure out what was stopping me. I remembered how I had solved writing problems in my old life in the country before my husband had died and wrecked me as surely as an earthquake takes down a building and turns it into a crumpled heap. I chose a time when there would be nobody around and when I had no pressing household tasks, and I would spend some moments in quiet contemplation in order to find my focus before putting on my jacket and with no object in mind other than to solve my problem, go out to walk the fields.

I emulated myself now, and did all these things, then set out for the nearest wild park at a time when there would be few people around. As I walked by myself, I concentrated and began a lawyerly cross-examination: I knew what the book was going to be about and how to write it, so that wasn't the problem. The problem was, I concluded to myself, that I could not find that writerly place inside myself, that steady inner state out of which the actual words and sentences begin to flow. I knew from past experience that I needed only to put my finger on the issues that were unsettling my long-honed ability to find that place, and so, as I moved down the treelined, asphalt path by the city reservoir I began mentally enumerating each one, some large, some trivial — one I wasn't aware of at the time, but later realized, being my own fear of failure — that was stopping me from finding that place from which the writing would come. I felt jittery, my mind skipping from one thought to another without resolving any one of them, so that in sheer exasperation with myself I stopped walking, looked up to the high tops of the trees that lined the trail on each side, and imagined myself throwing a stone at them as hard as I could.

The most obvious of the matters keeping me from being a writer again was everything on the morning's news: The

Russians had just annexed Crimea, and everybody was worried about what they might try next; a Boeing 777 with more than two hundred people on board had just disappeared in mid-flight, causing an endless round of helpless, baffled questioning and searching; a helicopter had crashed in downtown Seattle, killing the two people on board; and the day before, Los Angeles had a significant earthquake and aftershocks causing worry for West Coasters that it might be the prelude to the final Big One. All true, all horrifying, but unless you are personally, directly involved, it isn't hard, when you are about to begin a new book, to push that sort of thing out of your head.

I went on to my immediate family. True, there was serious illness, now that we are getting old, but there has been serious illness in my family since I was seven and the 1947 polio epidemic in Saskatchewan hit all four of us (the fifth wasn't born until 1949), nearly killing one and leaving her disabled for the rest of her too-short life. Worry about my sisters' ill health wasn't what was keeping me from writing. True, I had buried a forty-two-year-old niece two days previously. Since puberty, her life had been the cause of constant foreboding by everybody in the family, but now she was gone, safely underground, prayers said, tears wiped, her tragic life ended, or as close as it can be for the living who loved her. Not that, then.

Casting about for any other reason for my agitation, I thought of my own health. Thinking something *had* to be wrong (I'm old, am I not?), I had a checkup only a couple of weeks ago, and the doctor was amazed by my continuing good health. At seventy-three years, there seemed, annoyingly, to be nothing worth mentioning wrong with me. So what on earth was driving me crazy like this? Why was I so anxious and frightened? And why, no matter how carefully I dissected my thoughts and feelings, did the source of this worry refuse to reveal itself so that I could vaporize it with logic, or at least push it well enough away for a few hours each day so that I could sink into my already precious, new book?

I exhaled loudly, gazing around at the black-mottled cottonwood trunks shining white or a muted, hopeful green in the early spring sunshine, and higher up to the sky blazing through the fretwork of leafless finger-sized tree branches, then down to the melting snow at their bases. Never before had any issues stopped me from writing; even 9/11 stopped me cold for only a few days. I had shoved them far enough back that I could see in the distance that mental peace I was struggling for, but it still would not come. The longer I walked, pondering as I went, the more I began to understand that there was, accompanying me, distantly, threateningly, a silent, anonymous, dark mass. More relaxed now than when I had begun walking, it crept nearer, and, suddenly, I *knew* what it was.

Like West Coasters trying not to think about the one big earthquake threatening them, I had begun waiting for the Big One too: the cancer diagnosis, the stroke, the heart attack, the diagnosis of MS or Parkinson's or dementia or ALS. Every breath I took was at some level being examined by my subconscious to make sure it wasn't going to be my last, or the first of the disease that would, probably sooner rather than later, finish me off. But this one I already knew about, and had firmly — especially after my checkup where I was informed that my body was in near-perfect working order — dismissed as pointless, neurotic worrying. I no longer allowed myself such disquieting thoughts.

My book, the purpose of my stroll, vanished from my head as the realization hit me: the dark cloud blotting my personal horizon was Mr. Death himself, hanging around waiting for me to give in, to give up, to beckon him nearer just to get the endless uncertainty of the aged person over with. Simply by dint of being seventy-three, I knew, of course, that in the natural progression of things, he was closer than he'd ever been, and I knew — now, walking down that path and searching for that mental clarity and stillness out of which I write books — that without my noticing it, he had been tainting my every thought, desire, activity, and ambition. I had allowed it; on some level I was probably thinking I was being mature in accepting my condition of old age, but by doing so I was letting him stain and spoil my last years — not *last years*, I corrected myself — my *current years* — my life, right now.

I will not tell you that I resolved my quandary in the next few minutes. After all, reconciliation with mortality is the biggest struggle any old person has to deal with, except for those who deny and deny until the day they are dropped to their knees by a heart attack or a cancer diagnosis, when, in a perfect rage they go to their graves still gripping the edge of their coffins with their dead fingernails. Or the opposite: those who give up immediately and spend their last years in a semi-swoon, lying on the sofa with the television set on, being waited on by others, and checking carefully each morning to see if they are still alive; waiting, waiting, waiting for an obstinate death to come at last and claim them.

In my deepest part, I couldn't convince myself that starting another book was worth the effort, not with the Final Spectre breathing down my neck, nudging me now and then with a satiric elbow, and making me wonder at the value of any human endeavour, if obliteration was always, without exception, what it would come to. This dilemma was indeed too big for me to resolve, and so I returned to platitudes, to the centuries of them, all the ones that I had read and heard and that I knew legions of others my age were repeating to themselves: You're in good health; you'll live to ninety-five as lots of people do; you're only as old as you feel! But none of that was for me; I loathed the very sound of every one of those banalities; they infuriated me.

I had stopped walking, and now I started again, and slowly, floating or creeping from last year's damp grass and the sun on the trunks of the trees, and from something hovering in the air that came from what I couldn't say for sure, but that was nature itself, came the delicate, delicious scent of spring — even here, even in the heart of the city. By its fragrance moving through me, and with it all the springs of my life and all the ones yet to come, my fate — the same as everyone's, after all — seemed of less consequence and much less immediacy; you might say that my fate paled and retreated with gentle steps, wafting away until it dissolved into the fresh spring air. Death will come, but not today. Today I am *alive*.

A LIFE IN FRIENDS

Last night, I served a dinner that I had spent most of the day putting together for three of my friends. The original purpose of the occasion was for a fairly well-travelled woman in her fifties to hear about a certain trip she hoped to take, that a woman slightly older than I had already taken. The older woman, despite her age and health difficulties, has travelled a great deal, often to the most exotic and difficult places around, and shows no sign of stopping. Unfortunately, the fifty-year old friend had forgotten her hearing aids and couldn't hear much of what the older woman was telling her, and although she told the older friend this early on, I'm not sure the older friend was listening. I had also invited another woman, in her early sixties, because all of them had missed Paolo Sorrentino's film *The Great Beauty*, and I, thinking highly of the film and being in love with Rome, wanted them to see it too, and luckily, though it had left the local theatres, the film was available for one more day on my television service.

When I put the scallops into the heated pan, the hot butter splashed up, and I burned my hand, so that I spent the rest of the evening running back and forth to the fridge for ice to put on the burn. Then I spilled my glass of red wine, and it splattered over the favourite blouse of my sixty-year-old friend sitting at the end of the table, so she spent half an hour in the bathroom trying to get the stains out. I gave her my best exercise T-shirt to wear home, because it was the only top of mine that fit her; my lamb chop (beautifully cooked — by the way) skated off my plate and wound up on the off-white rug five feet away, leaving a greasy stain including a bit of mustard from my plate. These accidents happened because I was still recovering from cataract surgery, and I couldn't actually see anything close except as a blur. As for reaction to the film — the meal is best forgotten — one friend loved it as much as I did, maybe even more, one was approving, but not head over heels about it, and one (who had had a sleepless night) fell asleep and had to go home.

And yet, all in all, I think we had a good time. I know the evening wasn't a disaster, and either way, as I often tell myself, a night spent sitting around with friends is better than any night sitting around wishing I had somebody to sit around with. Having fun, although a good idea, isn't the goal at my age. All I want is the blessed comfort and pleasure of companionship with peers. I will not need skin grafts for my hand, nor will it have to be amputated; my friend got the stains out of her blouse; and when I can face it, I know that I can remove the mustard from the rug. Another plus: we are all still speaking.

Philosophers have been eloquent on the subject of friendship, but for the most part I haven't read them, my interest having always been more personal than intellectual, other than a foray into the writings of Donald Winnicott, the psychoanalyst and pediatrician, when I was writing a piece on creativity that involved thinking about children and play. When my son was a little boy, I was fascinated to see how tiny children seemed to recognize each other as creatures of the same ilk and to slowly approach each other even before they had language, much less knew the word "friendship." His father and I used to watch him playing together with other little children in sandboxes and on the grass, and it seemed that, for a long time, they didn't actually play *with* each other, but instead alongside each other, each doing his or her own thing. And yet, the presence of the other child seemed to be necessary for calm and satisfied play. This configuration must be where friendship begins, in proximity and companionship with someone perceived to be — even if only in the broadest terms, someone like oneself.

My first best friend was a girl who lived next door to us in a tiny French village, who, as far as I can remember, spoke little English while I spoke even less French. Yet for at least a year, we played together every day in true, shared delight. We both came from large families in which an individual child can become so easily lost in the near-chaos that is daily life when too many people are crammed into too small a house, and the parents receive a constant cacophony of competing demands. Although we children didn't know it, life was hard, although like most people in the village we had all our basic needs satisfied — food, roof, beds, and parents to make us stick to the most minimal of agendas. Because we lived in such small houses, when we weren't in school, we were sent outside to play, and thus, during the endless summers and on winter weekends, whenever the weather was good enough, we were outside, all ages thrown together, in winter skating on any frozen puddle we could find, and in summer, exploring the aspen forests at the end of the road or the grassy fields surrounding our village: nature was our playroom: green, wet, snowy and sunshiny, too hot, too cold; and yet, in memory an incomparable Eden.

I wonder, sometimes, if maybe I spoke more French than I remember (or at least understood more), and if my first best friend spoke more English. Nonetheless, talking played little part in our friendship; in my memory it was mostly about running through the long grass, or playing games together, usually with a crowd of other kids of all ages. And screaming: screaming seems to have been required for us to expand our small bodies into being alive in the world. So we screamed, and ran together, until one day my family and I moved to another town and I never saw her again.

I had many friends along the way, but none as significant as Margie, who became my best friend when we were twelve years old. Having a best friend then seemed to be a required stage of development: we all had one or wanted one, and even though we were also part of a gang of girls, and often boys, too, from our class, our primary relationship in life, the person with whom we did everything, and with whom we had the most intense exploratory conversations about our small world, was that other girl. Talk at last! Our world was full of conversation. I can't recall a word of it, have only a cloudy memory of much of it being about boys, although during that brief stage when we were hovering between childhood and a more grown-up world, I know those conversations were deeply important in my approach to that transition: I learned that I was not different from everybody else, that what I wanted was normal, and what she wanted was normal, too, that the future was bright (although brighter for her, I thought then), that we understood each other, and, by reflection, other girls, too.

But we were adolescents in a world where girls (and I suspect lots of the boys, too) did not know about sex — sex was a dark secret never more than faintly alluded to — and we certainly didn't talk about it. I recall how my mother's eyes darkened when one of my girlfriends suddenly announced to her, full of pride, as my mother stood at the ironing board, that a certain older boy had said she was "sexy." I was then forbidden to see her. "She's twelve years old!" my mother said in something deeper than mere dismay. But I think now that my mother pitied her, not that she found her disgusting or simply errant. Looking back, I think the girl was being sexually abused, who knew for how long, because her single-parent mother was frequently absent and ineffectual, and no one noticed or protected her, and my mother understood this, or at least suspected it and worried that I would be drawn into whatever was going on, too. And yet, my best friend and I never whispered about sex; we skirted that subject at all times, and though she may have known what it was all about, I, carefully, did not.

For most of a year, my new best friend, Margie, and I were intensely close, went everywhere together, including the Saturday afternoon black-and-white cowboy movies we liked. I have no idea now why, unless it was that it cost only a dime to get in, or maybe the simplicity of the plot lines appealed, with the posse always riding to the rescue, and the intensely masculine roles played by the male leads. They were the impossibly handsome Randolph Scott (I believe now outed as having been gay) and the singing cowboys, Roy Rogers and Gene Autry. But overnight, Margie grew tall, her pale little freckle-face smoothed itself into blue-eyed Irish prettiness, and boys — those same boys who had been my friends too — suddenly became mad about her. I was filled with envy, hurt, and a baffled humiliation bordering on shame, because, not having changed along with her, it seemed that whatever qualities of mine that had made us close friends had lost their value. Not only had I lost her, but she had moved to the centre of our social group, while I found myself suddenly shunted into the corner because I was still too much a little kid — me! The one who could think rings around the whole bunch — or so I must have told myself (and then wondered if that mattered, and worse, that it wasn't true), when I wasn't simply sunk in silent misery.

In almost no time, she found another best friend, a girl better suited to the person she had become, and that was one of the hardest times of my life up to then — not having a best friend, and knowing my old one was being unfaithful with another girl. In the fall, though, we went off to different high schools, and our paths never crossed again, and even though I often thought of her, I never saw her in the flesh again.

A good sixty years later, though, through mutual acquaintances, I heard what became of her, and I was so disconcerted by the news that I couldn't suppress a surprised, if mildly snotty laugh on being told. She had married a nice middle-class man, moved to the suburbs, had children, acquired a backyard swimming pool, and I can only guess must have lived happily ever after, while the latter, it's true, could never be said of me. And yet, finally, after about sixty years, I was mildly, ruefully, pleased to find myself, for a change, feeling superior to her! Because I didn't have a swimming pool? Because my life had been so varied and full of ups and downs, and was therefore more interesting, if also — in theory, anyway — more godawful?

I met my next closest female friend when I was nineteen, when we both met the men, themselves already inseparable friends, who became our first husbands. We were all university students, a foursome who did everything together when we weren't in classes, writing papers, or studying for exams. I have never laughed so hard in my life as we did together; I remember laughing so hard one night on a downtown street in Saskatoon that I simply couldn't stand up and collapsed to my knees onto the sidewalk. At first, Tamara and I were uncertain with each other — she seemed a marvellous creature to me, and she must have been a bit shy — although, in time, thrown together so much and facing the same problems concerning our relationships with our boyfriends, the barrier between us dissolved.

From that wonderful beginning, we became so close! We would never again in our lives have so much fun! But we sobered into two married couples, moved to different cities, and eventually, over the ensuing years, all divorced, my partner and me first, and fifteen or so years later she and her partner, each of us then living different lives, even for a time in different countries. Despite a lot of to-ing and fro-ing throughout middle age, including my long marriage to Peter while she was still married to her first husband, in our late seventies we two women live alone, while both men, to this day, predictably, live with new wives.

So many years later, Tamara and I still keep in touch from across the country, and when we are able to meet, it is as if we have never been apart. We shared not just that silly fun, and the wonder of first love, and our weddings and our babies, but also our pain, and nothing binds two women like shared, unassuageable pain. In the permanent absence of the two men who were also a part of that formative world, and as far away as she has been over many more years than those few we spent together, she nonetheless wove herself into my soul; without her, I would be a different, shallower person.

When I was just past thirty, divorcing and then divorced, and no longer remembering how to have a life without a husband, I met another friend. Katie had never been married, had travelled all over the world by then, had lots of relationships, and — something I especially admired and was very bad at myself — knew how to take care of herself. Then, I was in a frame of mind to break all the rules. She had never been good at following rules, and wasn't even aware of breaking them. I, to my annoyance, was the original rules-follower and a master at it. I suppose by then I was thinking: *and look how much good that did me.* This period, during the Second Wave of Feminism, meant we did a lot of things that I am amazed and embarrassed to think about now, but will admit to chortling inwardly about, before I straighten up and wipe that smirk off my face. My God! I felt alive and filled with possibility with her, instead of broken-hearted, grim, hopeless, suicidal, determined, and intensely achievement-oriented. To hell with all that! I'm here to have fun!

Well, sort of. I was a single mom, after all, and I had to deal with a divorce, money, a place to live, a job, the master's degree I was supposed to be working on, my son's education, and all the quotidian headaches of life. We cooked interesting dinners for our grad school friends; we threw fabulous, loud parties; we danced in a cloud of marijuana smoke (not that I ever touched the stuff) until we wore out our shoes and fell face down on the floor among all the other skinny, bead-wearing hippies with their unkempt beards and their wild hair and long, floaty skirts. Everybody's marriage was breaking up, partners were being exchanged and changed back again, and children suffered, in my opinion, terribly. I remember noticing that all these dope-smoking rule-breakers drifting around the country were actually young people from good homes, well brought up, middle class or higher, and the madness was all too ridiculous for words. But my friend and I held on to each other, wept on each other's shoulders, and every now and then she would announce firmly, "I'm off men!" She'd remain single for a week or two until male charm began again to attract her. As always, for me, men were elusive; at such times I often thought she had the right idea: life was easier without them.

Our friendship was based partly on our mutual availability. We didn't really need to talk about our pasts and our families. (I remember her meeting my aunt and uncle, and how surprised she was by how utterly French they were, although she knew that on my father's side, I had a French Canadian background.) Even now, I know almost nothing about her family, because she didn't talk much about them, and they lived far away. I often think that in those first years during and after my marriage breakup, without her I wouldn't have survived at all; I would have gone stark raving mad.

But our friendship had nothing to do with our sexuality, which we pursued elsewhere. I don't know if she would describe our relationship as one of love or not, but there was an empathy between us as women, that my husbands have never equalled, no matter how much love I shared with them. That marital relationship, as Montaigne says, is fraught with so many things: mandatory continuing association, the sexual component, and the children who become for most of us its focus, none of which exists in a true friendship between women.

I am trying to locate the difference between the friendship I had with this woman and what I have had with two husbands: the lack of the sexual component, and the intensity of marriage at the beginning, as if the married couple is one person and everyone else is invisible. Byron wrote that "friendship is love without his wings"; without his *madness*, I think, would be closer to the truth. Now that romantic love is over for me, I think of it as a divine madness. At the time, as young brides do, I often used to say that my first husband was my best friend, but comparing what we had together to what I have with my women friends, I realize that the relationships differ. My husband and I would not have been friends if we were not first sexually attracted to each other. (Montaigne declares women incapable of having both a sexual relationship and a friendship as well, but by friendship he seems to be referring approvingly to older-male-younger-male mentorships as well as the sexual relationships that the Greek upper classes once had.)

As well, now I see the things I didn't like about him, but I didn't see them then, while any woman I was close to either didn't have faults that mattered to me, or I could look away from them, the difference being that I — not stricken by that kind of love — could *see* them, while, besotted with him, I was blind to my husband's shortcomings. No, I think now that my first husband and I were not friends at all. We loved each other, but our friends were other couples, or individuals of our own sex. Possibly in a lesbian relationship based on mutual attraction, followed by love, you can also be genuine friends as the Greeks asserted — or at least, as Montaigne did.

In *Much Ado About Nothing*, Shakespeare wrote, "Friendship is constant in all other things/Save in the office and affairs of love." What was true in the late sixteenth century, and despite the Second Wave of Feminism, remains true today. I came from an era where the single most important goal in life was not to grow spiritually and emotionally and develop ourselves, but to acquire a husband. I can't remember any forces seriously suggesting otherwise, and even your mother, who may well have suffered for twenty or thirty or more years in a marriage that made her deeply unhappy, would take that notion for granted, and would keep a weather eye out for the relationship that might turn into a marriage for her daughters, if not for her sons. When I announced to my mother triumphantly that I was getting married, without a beat passing, she said, "No, you're not!" which I find both gratifying and shocking. Her automatic reaction of seemingly wanting to protect me makes me laugh now. So, I dispute the idea — I know many will disagree — that a romantic spouse or partner can also be a good friend.

Although my best friend and I were heading toward real maturity, we were still young, and we were still competitive about men. We didn't have outright rivalries — we cared too much for each other for that — and we tried not to covet the same man, nor to blame each other for males preferring one of us over the other. I think if both of us had fallen genuinely in love with the same man, one of us would have gone away to another town or city or maybe even country, rather than launching into a full-fledged battle. True friends, in our genuine mutual sympathy, make sacrifices for each other.

We both carried on as singles for about a year until the madness slowed, and then faded away like the last coils of pot smoke when the party has ended. I married again, and during those first years, when we lived far from each other but kept in contact, she met the man who became her life partner. So, the world moved on, but my joyful memory of that friendship and my feeling of tenderness toward her will never leave me, just as the memory of my first abortive love relationship that came to nothing will also never leave me. I puzzle over that early love, think *if I'd just done this, or that* — but I don't puzzle over my friendship. Friendship, I think, is less complicated than love.

But she is still my friend, deeply and ineradicably so, and now, nearly fifty years later, whenever we are in each other's vicinity, we get together. Although we don't talk about those days, the base of affection in our relations with each other is precious to us both. Because, I often think, although I don't know if she would agree or not — note to self: ask her — that that period, with the parties and the dancing and the relationships, was really all about allaying suffering more than it was about hope, or even the fun itself; I sought much of it to crush my despair.

I HADN'T REALIZED until I began writing this short list of certain friends how very important friendship has been in my life. No wonder I was so sad in all those thirty-plus years when I was living on the ranch with Peter and couldn't seem to find or make a friendship that would last, so that in place of it, I dug so deeply into scholarship, wandering in nature, and writing. True friends would have made those years so much easier, but among the women of the countryside, our mutual distrust, the huge differences in how and where we were brought up, mostly made deep friendships impossible.

During all those years I lived on the ranch and hay farm with my husband, I was mostly without friends. Nearly thirty-three years without a close friend, other than sporadically, now and then, for short periods that would end either with the new friend, having come from elsewhere, leaving again, or her discovery or mine that we weren't compatible after all. I didn't understand then what I was doing wrong. All I knew was that I wasn't liked, that the local women turned away from me, even to the extent that they sometimes shamefully piled on. The more I published, the more the distance increased between me and everybody else, and this hurt me profoundly and made me question myself to such an extent that it's a wonder I didn't leave.

During all those years, doubting myself more and more, I often had to remind myself that this was the first time in my life I couldn't find a friend, that friends came naturally to me when I was in an environment where I was an equal. I was a loner simply by living there (although I had some companionship from two other women in the same boat), and for many years I had to find ways to occupy my spare time that were engrossing in themselves; I had to learn how to be my own friend, although that platitude offends me. I withdrew, got proud, said to myself that I would remain myself no matter what it cost me. I was tough, I said to myself, and being right, I would survive when everything else went to hell around me.

So, friends I mostly did not have, and no family around to support me, either. But then, had I been accepted and had many friends in those years; that is, women in my age group who shared my interests, I feel certain that I would have been too busy with ranch work, house and yard work, and a full social life to do much more than dabble in writing. There needn't be a choice between friendship and commitment to a vocation, but if years pass, many, many years, and that rounded social life with close friends fails to develop, there is no point in bemoaning that lack of balance. But, without a close dear friend, the heart grows cold; it distances itself from human warmth, and it finds what comfort it can in true work and in ideas.

When I first came to live in Calgary fifteen months after I buried my husband, I had no friends here, and aside from my relatives, hardly any acquaintances. And I was caught in a state of confusion, grief, and emotional turmoil. My anxiety was extreme, getting around in Calgary was terrifying, and I think for the first two years my blood pressure must have been constantly elevated and my heart rate faster than normal. I desperately needed friends to help me through that challenging period of transition so that I didn't have to rely so heavily on my overburdened son. Not that I imagined friends taking care of me, but only that they could advise me, sympathize with me, and give me courage. I imagined how, just as they would have made country living easier, they could make the whole effort of learning this new way of living easier. Imagine laughing with her over the idiot (his own car so crumpled on every side it was a wonder he could drive it) who stopped in traffic to yell at me for some imaginary crime, instead of going home and crying and being afraid to drive for a week.

One woman I already knew, although not well, took me under her wing. Sara, one of the busiest people I've ever met — a retired person, of course — did everything she could to help me through this immensely demanding period of my newness to the city, along with my struggle adjusting to being a widow, and to the trauma of growing old. She often invited me out to lunch or dinner and to meetings and other events, and, sensitive to my uneasiness with city driving, gave me more rides than I can count. Even though I hadn't thought of her as a friend when I left the country, I had lost confidence that anybody new would ever want me for a friend, or I had become so experienced in receiving a veiled insult or put-down that now I was afraid to approach people. No matter how eagerly I accepted her ten thousand kindnesses, and although I was intensely thankful to her, I was also simply puzzled at her interest in me.

Most of all, though, I will never get over my embarrassment at the way, in my dire emotional straits, she let me talk and talk, and talk and talk. How infinitely patient she was with me. Even when I knew what I was doing, I couldn't seem to stop, until finally I must have talked myself out, and finished with that part of my adjustment. At the same time, other parts of my new life continued to develop, but in none of it was there anyone as generous, indeed as noble, as Sara was.

Once I emerged from this period of perhaps taking advantage of her kindness rather than being able to be an equal friend to her, I took some time to sort out how I should understand our relationship. But one day, in my woundedness and mistrust, I considered the friendship from every angle, and phoned her, saying a trifle indignantly, as if answering all the women in my old life who didn't think I was friendship material, "Why shouldn't I have somebody nice for a friend?" She might have laughed at that — it does sound a bit crazy now — but, undaunted, feeling sure of myself finally, I asked: "Will you come over for coffee?" She said yes, and came at once, and that was a turning point not just in our relationship, but in my new life. Through her undaunted, even dogged, persistence in supporting me, or, more accurately, in putting up with me, I had at last regained some confidence in myself as a person worthy of friends. Eleven years later, we are still close, and although our busy lives mean we see less of each other than at first, she forms the solid foundation of my new life.

How many times have I heard or read older women saying that their friends are the most important people in their lives, that without friends they don't know how they would have survived, that women in mid-life should do everything they can to make friends and to hang onto them? You don't really understand the wisdom of this sentiment, or at least, I didn't, until you are an old woman, whether living alone or not, when the people whose very existence frames and gives your life meaning are stripped to nobody. You remember your friends then, going back to your childhood; you remember the intensity of some of those relationships, how validating they were, even life-giving to you, and imagine — I suppose — that they were the stuff of youth and can never be that way again.

And yet, I have an apparently odd habit, that often surprises people: I have kept track of my friends going back to my initial days in university, but mostly from the time when I returned to the university in my early thirties. My small success as a writer, something far in my future when I went to live in the country in 1976, gave me the chance to travel around Canada, every now and then to cities where my old best friends lived. So, of course I looked them up and sometimes stayed with them in their homes, or went out to dinners and lunches with them and even on little trips around their cities to see the sights. These visits restored my confidence, and back at my friendless country home, I felt that I was, after all, a worthy friend.

Through thick and thin, year after year, I sent my old friends notes, occasionally talked to them on the phone, and then, when the technology arrived, we have kept in touch by email. I even keep in sporadic touch with a girl from my Grade 8 class in Saskatoon more than sixty-five years ago.

I love knowing what became of her, and what she is doing now, and what she is thinking about. That we both wound up with husbands born to the agricultural life, who took us into it, amuses us. Why does she matter to me, I ask myself? She was part of a significant year in my life, and as a child, she was warm, kind, and generous, and still is. It makes me feel good to know her now, as if I am in my old age gathering all the loose ends of my life and pulling them tight around me. Ah, yes, that happened; I exist, I existed even then.

I had this unarticulated feeling that my old friends and I have a soul connection, and that to break our connection would violate some unspoken promise of what we had once meant to each other. My old friends and I share an unspoken layer of knowing — even as we talk quietly about this or that. Perhaps our conversation would sound to others much as it would if we'd known each other only a year or so. But to us, it is not like that at all. What began as something casual and unplanned — we double-dated, or we lived in the same neighbourhood, or we sat near each other in a university class — grew over the years into a friendship, and then, as more years passed, and we talked maybe once a year or every two years, and perhaps visited again briefly, our friendship has turned into a kind of love. In a crisis, we can, if we need to, turn to each other for that understanding ear so necessary to keep away the always-threatening hopelessness of the old.

The very old, having lost every single person who knew them as children, as young people, and in their middle age, at times feel they have lost their very validation as human beings. I dream of the dead often, quite possibly for part of every single night — my parents, my two dead sisters, my husband, and two male friends. But when I awaken, I am not saddened, instead I wake feeling as if — no, *knowing* — that they are still very much alive somewhere, even if only in my psyche, and I am comforted knowing that they are still with me.

I believe also that once a true friend, forever a friend, to death a friend — how could it be otherwise — and it would take some pretty serious lying or meanness or the discovery that the relationship was based on a deliberate inauthenticity on the part of one to put an end to it. I have recently reconnected with a friend from the days before I married Peter and am so happy to find that we share the same empathy that we had forty years ago.

When I was young, my friendships gave me a way of growing up: our closeness, our discussions, our complaints to each other about our families, or even, sometimes, repeating what our mothers had said to each other as the fount of all wisdom. We didn't really know that we would be women one day, or what that meant, but we were helping each other grow towards it. We were not only providing a bulwark against the sorrows and cruelty of the world, but we were teaching and especially *nurturing* each other. Our mothers belonged to a different part of our lives, or were dead, and we had our pride where our siblings were concerned, or we had quarrelled too much with them in childhood for them to be the close confidantes our girlfriends were. And in most of our cases, men had turned out inadequate to attend to our emotional needs. In your seventies, it is unlikely that your mother is still alive to comfort you: where else might we find the nurturing that all of us, sometimes, require?

So, I moved to Calgary, and family remembered me and my new solitude, and invited me to dinners and barbecues, and even, a couple of times, to hockey games where a talented young relative was playing. I had a couple of acquaintances when I arrived, and through them I met other women, and bit by bit I managed to build a small network of friends and acquaintances with whom I could do things. They are my social life and provide me with most of the emotional intimacy so necessary to the female soul. And yet, my relationship with these new friends, wonderful as they are, is different and less intimate than the ones with the women whom I first knew in my youth.

Of course, now I have learned how to manage most of my own problems — or more interestingly, perhaps I don't really have big problems anymore: no difficult spouse, no troubled children, no serious money worries; I am beyond career failures or heartbreak — and don't need a friend to help me manage any of that. Now I need companionship, serious conversations about life, a willingness to talk about our own less-than-stellar futures, someone with whom to share interests such as literature and the other arts, and a strong sense of mutual empathy whether we talk about it or not. My friends and I struggle determinedly not only to keep ourselves occupied doing interesting and enjoyable things, but to help each other in this. It turns out that in old age I can finally see that friends are never superfluous (or, at least, not for long), but are *and have always been* an essential component of the good life.

At my youngest sister's "celebration of life" after her death at only sixty-four, one of the guests was an eighty-nine-year-old woman who for many, many years, although younger than our mother, who by then had been dead for twenty-seven years, had been a close friend of hers. She reminded us with tears in her eyes that our dear lost little sister back in 1949 had been named after her. We wept over our losses even though nearly a generation separated us, and we were close only because our mother had cared so much for her, and she for our mother, a heartfelt bond that couldn't be dissolved even by death. And why did we both cry? (When I was young enough in those days to have babysat the sixty-year-old daughter who brought her to the celebration of life?) I remembered when I was nine, coming home from school the day my mother brought our new little sister home from the hospital, and Mom was sitting in the living room, the baby asleep in her cot beside her, deep in an intimate conversation with her friend from across the street, the now eighty-nine-year-old in the wheelchair.

It wasn't just my sister's death; it was also my mother's death. I was weeping for that life we had once been a part of, so many years ago, when my now-dead sister was a baby, and we were families that lived across the street from each other, and their husbands — my mother's and her friend's — were both alive, and the world was alive too, with possibility and hope. We were weeping for the cruelty of life — as well, she had been widowed twice and I once — for the human fate that was now inexorably before us both. Our age difference was fifteen years, almost a full generation, but in that moment it didn't matter, and I think that in that moment, I now an old woman, my mother's dear friend became in some way my friend, as had her daughter. I said to her, as we held each other, "Your presence here has given this event meaning that it wouldn't have had without you," and I meant it, and mean it still.

How right the rock stars were when they sang, "Love is not enough" (although they meant something else: compassion, money, planning, execution). But they were right in matters of the human soul. Love may be absent, occupied, vague; it may be impure, confused, selfish, vacillating. Friends fill in the gaps, are there when you need them; they understand, or try hard to understand, and whether they succeed or fail, the effort alone, the sympathetic ear, makes being alive easier. In old age, friendship can be at its best, the relationship where empathy is complete, and care for the other — not a relative, not a love object — is at its purest.

THIS STRANGE VISIBLE AIR

When I was twenty-three and the exhausted mother of a sleepless first baby, I lay down one evening for a nap, and instead of finding the blessed oblivion I longed for, found myself in another universe. Here, our baby lay sleeping in his carriage on the lawn and under the rich green foliage of the gnarled elms that lined our backyard. This was our yard, our grass, our trees, our sidewalk, our rickety once-white picket fence, but this homey familiar scene was surrounded by, occurred within air that, though translucent, was pebbled, or textured. I could see the air. The entire scene, including the air, was utterly still; not the stillness of the living room when you first come home, nor the stillness of a crowd watching something odd in the sky, but a stillness that was itself alive.

Nothing ticked or moved, no voice spoke, the scene and its meaning were whole, which I saw at once; and I saw also at once that it was inarguable, it simply *was*. Everything in the universe is made of the same material: the trees, the grass, the air, my baby, too — everything except the narrow, chipped cement path that had no life. It was *dead*. All that was alive — this strange, visible air, the trees, the grass, and the baby — were not presented as "people/not people, animate/not-animate, conscious/not-conscious, more meaningful/less meaningful," but as all of the same piece. Nowhere, not ever in my life, had I seen such beauty, beauty that only the cement path marred.

WHEN WE SPEAK of our love of nature and our need to be in it as often as we can, we talk of the peace we find there, we talk of its beauty, and of the pleasure of being lost in nature's solitude, even of the promise of freedom to be found there, while none of these attributes are quantifiable or even fully definable. I have wanted to tear apart those too-facile words and to try to find what they really mean; that is, to find what the deeper and more powerful draw of nature is, and what the feeling of being sustained and heartened by it is, if also finding in it an unanswerable grief and profound yearning for what, we don't know, try as we might to name it. It is as if we dream of the day when nature will finally speak to us, tell us what it causes us to long for.

In my writing, I have struggled to answer this question for myself, not finding the answers in the work of scientists, naturalists, or hobbyists, not even in Thoreau, Aldo Leopold, Wallace Stegner, Annie Dillard, or other famous writers about nature or aspects of it, finding often only a new way to state the question, or an obstinate refusal to so much as look at it. Perhaps the answer lies beyond such writings or speeches, even that of theologians, and probably also philosophers, although sometimes poets touch on it. I am none of these.

I observed, during my thirty-three years on the remote ranch and hay farm belonging to my husband and to me, that whenever visitors came, what they most wanted was to be outside on the land. As the day outside wore on, their faces became flushed, they laughed a lot in a bubbling-up, child-like way, in a kind of ebullience that is usually otherwise induced mostly by cocktail parties. They exuded happiness, even joy, their much-battered souls had undergone soothing, even healing. Their day out of the city wilds and inside the landscape had been a sojourn in a kind of paradise.

The sense of a looming, healing presence, I think, permeates all of us when we are in nature. We become specifically aware of it if we are not focused on birding, not cracking open rocks, not hiking X miles or searching for something — a particular grass, butterfly, or lichen — but simply *being* there. Especially if we can also stop the constant whirring of the consciousness, the questioning, the whining, the anger — at least, these are the things I have to stifle — and learn to be alone, to quietly walk, and listen, and see. In fact, to see what is always there, but that we can only otherwise sense or dimly perceive or fail to perceive — an oxymoron, a contradiction, a sortie into another world than the rational and logical — even scientific — one in which we commonly live.

Scientists have given many essential reasons why we must save as much wild nature as possible, from preserving watersheds for safe water sources, to guaranteeing a steady supply of nutritious food and medicines, to ensuring we have clean air to breathe. I accept them all as true and necessary, but I insist that there is a more ancient, perhaps even an eternal reason, for the human need to exist in nature, and thus why we must save all that we can.

Now I am seventy-nine years old, and my sojourn on this planet is nearly over. For more than fifty years, I contemplated a vision of the universe, trying to understand it as the background to how I live, and to find a way to integrate it into my ordinary, daily life, and mostly failing. Not long ago, early on a chilly Sunday morning, I walked the path that winds through the trees at the Weaselhead Natural Area on the edge of my city, which becomes wilderness: the wetlands, then prairie, then the foothills and on into the unvanquished, towering Rocky Mountains. I was alone; the natural area was quiet, even though Calgary droned to the north, east, and south of me. I stopped walking to savour the beauty and whatever delicate thing emanates from a forest that is still and empty of people.

It was then that I saw again the fabric of the universe; once again it became visible to me, textured, so as not to be invisible, this time the palest sandy pink. What had so gently become visible (or my vision mysteriously cleared so that I could see it) is always present. Within this coloured, motionless, indeed, sentient air, the trees stood, the shrubs and bushes, the grasses, all still and soft, and I saw that, at that moment, I walked within nature, and I, myself, existed as part of the benign fabric of the universe. Time passed. I walked delicately on, immersed in wonder.

I think we are, all of us, even though we don't actively know it, working out of this vision that for me, and much of the world for millennia, is a fundamental truth. I think that all of us have had this truth implanted in us in the moment of our conception. Or perhaps it needs no implantation, because we are made of it, but we forget this knowledge, lose track of it, and need to be reminded.

Without wild nature, even the degree of it we can access in cities, to remind us who we humans are, our souls thin and fade and may even shrivel and disappear. In nature, we rediscover and reinvigorate ourselves as human beings, and stretch ourselves, easily, in great relief and delight, to rediscover the experience that, to our immense impoverishment, we are close to losing in modern life. In nature, we feel the joy and the grief contained in remembering once again who we are.

PASSING THROUGH

One of the first things young people should be told is that one day they will be old. When you're old, in dismay and disbelief you will ask yourself a dozen times a day, *How on earth did I wind up like this?* looking around your empty apartment at the light coming in through the windows, spreading like clear water across the threadbare rug; hearing the low drone of the radio in the other room; thinking, I need to talk to someone — a certain someone — reminding yourself then that he or she is dead.

If you're smart, you'll think of the past, the rooms full of people, the noise from voices calling, chattering, laughing, crying, the streets, too, full of people walking by, pausing to tie a shoelace, to sit down at the sidewalk tables across the street from your apartment. You will think: *that time in Paris, the crippled boy in Addis Ababa, the cold water of the lake as you swam to the raft and clambered up, water pouring off you, you, shivering and elated.* Then it is easy to remember that you are old and that is the past, and it is gone forever and will not return, not even after you have crossed over into the next place. Forever!

Then you will remember that most of us end this way and that most of us would think we are the lucky ones: *consider the alternatives,* we remind ourselves, until the day comes when all we want is the alternative. Yet we are tired of how we have wound up; we see no future anyone would want, we begin to look forward to a new way of being, or a new space in which to be. But, still, you ask, where am I going? Where is this story going? What is its meaning? At this point, you always set aside the book you're not reading, go to the kitchen, and make yourself a cup of coffee. Or wash the kitchen floor.

You begin to realize, too, that what others think of as the past is not what you think of: Desert Storm? No: Dieppe, Dachau, a divided Berlin, the airlifting of food into the city, the bombing of Dresden and London, the young returning soldier in his thick woollen uniform and his putties, his blank eyes, sitting in your mother's kitchen. Those world events are real to you. Desert Storm is a comic book. Even the bad dreams are old now; they don't come anymore. Instead, sometimes you dream of the next world, of getting there: climbing the cliff to the light above, or the vast white marble staircase to the not-quite-seen city in the air, or else of the spacious, uncluttered, beautiful house filled with a perfect stillness.

In the last bad dream you remember having, you were in a temple. In the temple, built of dark granite and rose and black marble, a man was carrying you down a hallway with gleaming floors, between widely spaced rows of high pillars. You passed tables, slabs of polished rock that looked like Incan or Mayan sacrificial tables, perhaps, where hearts were cut from living bodies, or like the wide altar tables in vast Roman cathedrals on which bread and wine were incarnated as flesh. But despite the cleanliness and the readiness, ancient holy rituals were no longer carried out there. A polished, empty temple out of which you were being carried with tenderness, expelled, through the great hall, down the few wide steps, outside to the sun-bleached desert beyond, where the man set you gently down on the flat hard sand dotted here and there with scrub. Was it even a bad dream? What was it?

Asking these questions, over and over again, you begin to see what old is about. That, and going over and over again your many — your thousands, no, tens of thousands, of sins and transgressions, unkindnesses, cruelties, mistakes and failures, deceptions, lies, and half-truths — until finally, when you reach the point where you accept that you can do nothing about a single one of them. They exist only in the past, a past that cannot either be retrieved and improved, or changed. You grow much older, you can feel the light going out of your eyes, and you know you are near the end, because some kind of truth, of necessary knowledge, is surfacing in this endless repletion of your sorrows and your irreparable sins. The knowledge of the unforgiven, unassuaged damage you did. Even the day when your weariness precludes your going over them again, even as your eyes fill with tears and your hand goes up in a fist, your knuckles knocking your forehead. *Woe is me; mea culpa* . . . what good is all that? You would stop if you could, but then it stops of itself, and you feel that you have perhaps advanced a micro-miniscule of a step into what you do not know, but have needed to know. But you also think that — original thought — life is vastly, intimately cruel, and there is no cure for it, not for any of us.

Sometimes, voices speak to you. You recognize them as different from the dead spouse, or children, or parents, or close friends. You don't know who they are or where they come from, but you recognize that they mean well, they try to say important things to you, the right thing, even though the remark is so simple you want to forget it. They say, *What? Are you trying to be a saint?* with a touch of humour. They say, solemnly, *this, too, is illusion.* You recognize that everything is simple, very simple, ridiculously simple, and has been staring you right in the face the whole time, while you spent your life convinced that everything is so much more complicated and beyond your true understanding. No, it was there all the time, and, worse, you knew it.

You were just confused by all the noise: the iPads and iPhones and Macs and Apples; by the celebrities and their shenanigans and that absurd, shameless new president and his model wife and his children by three different women; by your own jobs and lovers, and the spouses and the children and the siblings and grandparents and in-laws and neighbours and the bills to pay and the insurance and taxes. Deep inside the whole time was the right thing, but you couldn't hear it over the din. You couldn't hear it over the whine of your own uncertainty and the endless howl of your desire. You couldn't hear it over your own rage and grief and jealousy and envy.

How do you know, others ask? You'll know it too, when you get to be my age. You better hope to live long enough to know all this that I have written, because the situation you would have to be in to have the knowledge when you were younger would be so tumultuous and death riddled. You would not want to find it out through despair; you would be better to find it out by passing through the fire of life and not dying. You would be better then, to have the time to think. Then you would see all your ideas about life for what they really are. Nonsense. Hogwash. Layers of lies upon lie upon lie.

You sometimes think that if you are to find your way through the false self to the real self, you might find that we are identical — all of us — identical in our souls and in our spirits. Like everybody else who is not a Buddhist, you don't like that thought one bit, do you? But gender stuff, sexuality? You don't know. The other day you were watching a spy show on television, a scene in which a pack of FBI agents swarmed through a suspect's apartment searching for evidence and took apart the wiring and even melted the ice cubes, when a female agent pulls aside the quilt covering the bed where a young couple have been making love. In that second, as she studies the creased and stained once-white sheet, some things flashed through your brain so fast that, although you mostly followed them at the time, later you remembered the sequence of thoughts only once and would never again be able to recover it.

But in that instant, you saw that you had always tried hard to protect your sexuality, protect it in some pristine, private, and almost spiritual way. You knew just as quickly that this protectiveness came from your very early childhood rape or abuse (you will never know exactly what it was, only that you screamed and screamed afterward and were never the same child again ever, it affected you so profoundly and altered forever whom you might have been). You also knew that your sense of privacy had nothing to do with boyfriends, lovers, husbands, or even childbirth and babies. You would say that perhaps you did always know the effect of that abuse on you; that is, you've known since you were sixty, but what you did not know was that almost Roman-soldier-like part of you, stoic, pure and white, that wished always to stay that way — always, into adulthood and well beyond, even into this old, old age of yours. Maybe only now, as an old woman, you begin to understand the fear of the divine power of the feminine as the cause of male aggression toward women.

Or, you wonder, is "power" the word you mean? No, it is *essence. The essence of the feminine, that owes the male nothing and asks for nothing from him,* and stands side by side and equal with the male essence. (This in a world where women are everywhere routinely abused and denigrated.) And so, you have at last isolated one potent theme in your life, that of the mostly latent power women have; you are surprised; you are somewhat in awe; you are satisfied to put it away now. One more item understood and settled.

You remember that sensible old people and their younger relatives, the social workers and psychologists, tell you that *you mustn't live in the past.* But now you know that for old people like you, the past and the present coexist; there is no separation between them, not in any meaningful way: for old people, the past is the present, and that's a good thing. We are elders; we work to integrate the past to achieve a new, higher-level understanding.

When you got out of bed this morning, you happened to glance at the calendar (you were looking for spring, as if the calendar would be a better guide than the view out your window at the city rooftops) and realized then that in two weeks your new book would be out and the emotional roller coaster would start again. You think this book will be your last, you know that everything is coming to an end all too soon, and the part of you that harbours regrets feels remote. You are exhausted at the thought of carrying on.

Having a goal in life is tiring, pursuing the Holy Grail of getting-it-right-at-last, of having an ambition so great — if always completely unspeakable — that rivals God's. You're old — eighty this year — and you don't think you can keep up the pace required of you. But you also cannot drop out, although you think you can dial down the speed a bit. Although you recognize the futility, the meaninglessness that you couldn't even consider when you were younger and first became afflicted with this disease of achievement.

And yet, if you could live this life over again, you would do it all again. You would have no regrets; you would run around screaming out loud about your affliction. You would ask for no mercy, you would . . . yeah, like hell you would. And yet, there isn't any other way to live that you can see, at least, not for people like you, who — although not born with it — have a permanent hole inside that comes from childhood wounding, one that can never be properly filled or repaired, and that weeps, moans, and wails for attention all their lives. The unfillable hole that drives ambition, achievement. Or that might be said, in the end, to be the gift of a life.

PERCEPTIBLE LIGHT

Some months ago, during a close examination of my eyes, a young optometrist told me that I had macular degeneration "just barely starting" in both of them. She stood with her back to me, fiddling with something, speaking in a low, light voice that signified to me that either she wasn't sure if she should tell me or not, or wasn't sure how to tell me. Maybe I was the first person she had ever had to give such bad news. I paid her no mind, because I knew that I would somehow escape this verdict. I was then almost seventy-eight years old, so before the condition could take full effect, I would be dead. Case closed, as they say on TV.

I left her examination room as jauntily as I had entered it, even though I had been having trouble with my right eye ever since my cataract surgery four years earlier, and there seemed no explanation for it. I couldn't rub away the haze or wash it out of my eye or off the lens of my glasses, or blink it away, and to be truthful, I sometimes missed letters in words when I was reading and had to go back, where, miraculously, the missing letters would reappear. Sometimes I would see things or people at the edge of my vision when there was no one or nothing there, all of which I had told the optometrist. That's why she did the deeper examination resulting in her, I thought, faintly weird behaviour as she made the pronouncement of my diagnosis.

For at least a full month, her diagnosis seemed to me distant and unreal, forgettable because it wouldn't come to pass during my lifetime. I was still vigorous and often told I was unusually young-looking for my age. I was also still stubbornly working as a writer, still publishing, even though small voices in my head were whispering to me that I was done, that my time as a writer had passed, that I no longer understood the world, and anything relevant I might have to say was relevant only to us, the nearly dead (my occasional, not entirely whimsical term for my age group — people approaching eighty and over). I knew people with MS, or COPD or Parkinson's disease, or the beginnings of some kind of dementia, many of them younger than I; so clearly, I thought, that kind of catastrophe wasn't in the cards for me. These thoughts were evidence, nonetheless, that the optometrist's diagnosis was working away below my full consciousness.

I mentioned this verdict to an acquaintance — odd that I would choose to tell her and not my family — who lent me a twenty-year-old book on the subject, written by an ophthalmologist, who, in middle age, had developed the problem himself. By the time I had finished his book, the thought began to sink in that I had to accept I was facing the end of my life as I knew it. My next thought was to look around for help, somebody to tell this to. But it was summer, and most of my close friends were off on vacations, and not many months before, my family had moved a couple of thousand miles away; and anyway, I thought it far too soon to burden them with the news of my diagnosis. I was alone and could think of no one I wanted to phone to talk with about the news that I was about to go blind at a time when I was already old and losing abilities and continuously wondering who would care for me when I could no longer care for myself, and was surreptitiously considering available options, as were many of the single, aging women (from early sixties to over ninety) with whom I was acquainted. When we talked about the problem as to where we would end our lives, we tried not to sigh audibly, and gazed absently out the window, our expressions carefully neutral.

Already, as with many old people, I was having trouble filling my evenings and weekends with activities with my friends, a number of whom still had husbands or grown-up children and their families nearby, and who scheduled time with friends only when their partners and families weren't available. And now, to be blind as well! I, who had spent my life reading, studying, going to films, sometimes painting, and staring at a computer screen as I wrote book after book, more than twenty in all. How would I fill all those endless solitary hours when I could not see? An unexpected rage engulfed me, and I spent an entire weekend lost in it, clomping down park pathways, trying to breathe through its heat, trying not to have my head explode while it churned with incoherent thoughts, on fire with indignation, and violent half-images that seared my brain, and that I killed at once, only to have others appear before I mentally bashed them out of sight.

I consoled myself with the thought that not being able to see is actually quite a wonderful thing, and that friends and family would rally around and buy my groceries for me, and guide me on walks and take me to the symphony and chamber concerts. Blindness is good for the soul! Hah! I could think of nothing worse, except maybe suffering from severe debilitating chronic pain, or dying in a dungeon for a crime you didn't commit. I suppose I meant that, in terms of who I am, within a normal North American life, I could think of nothing worse: to be completely alone to deal with this life-changing and inalterable verdict; to realize my working life as a writer after forty years was over, and I did not know what I would do in place of it; to realize that almost certainly I was not going to die before the full force of the condition hit; to know that I was caught in a vice of destiny's making, and I did not even have anyone to confide in. I mean, you don't tell the women you always see in the grocery store about your scary diagnosis, or your across-the-hall neighbour with whom you have a tenuous relationship at best, or the woman with whom you have lunch once a month. Although I had two sisters left, one was in Europe for the summer (albeit in a wheelchair) with her family, and the other had a serious long-term illness, and, in any case, both lived far away from me. As for my close friends, they had troubles of their own, and didn't need to add mine to their burdens.

One evening I noticed that the pill container I used when I travelled had the days of the week written on it in braille — at least, I assumed those little bumps, each set different, were braille, and was surprised and pleased. A glimmer of hope entered the blackness of my fury and near-despair. I had bought the container where I buy most of the things I need for my daily life, at the co-op down the street, and not in some specialized store for the blind. Okay, so I would have to learn braille. My head was clearing. I began to try to imagine how I would live with this disability, practically, step by step.

Occasionally, when I couldn't sleep, I tried to put on my bedside radio and find the CBC without turning on the light, running my fingers over the buttons, counting, trying to locate the right one. I closed my eyes, too, and concentrated on the meaningful sounds, a musical phrase, a few vowels and consonants in different voices coming softly, intimately from the radio in the 3:00 a.m. hush. Or I searched for my glasses or my keys with my eyes closed, testing how well I could navigate my own home without sight. Already a sight-less world was closing in around me, and I saw how intimate it would be, how solitary, and, possibly in some way I wasn't yet sure about, how blessed. But I also could see myself growing more and more careless, showing up in my summer navy and white polka-dot pants with a plaid shirt, not the plain white one I thought I had on, my hair ravaged and unsightly, eventually throwing myself in front of a commuter train. Whoa!

I reminded myself over and over again that if I had macular degeneration, according to the ophthalmologist whose book I had read, I would always see light, would never be in total darkness. I thought of books I had read about the blind heroes: Helen Keller, Jacques Lusseyran, people whose breathtaking adaptability interwove with unquenchable bravery, and despite my anger, I was inspired by them. I knew damn well I didn't have their courage. I was already worn out with the endless uncertainty and never-ending troubles of being alive.

Not only did I not tell anyone for at least a month, possibly two, I didn't do anything about the diagnosis, at first thinking that nothing could be done anyway, so why bother. I suspect that at a deep level, I still thought the problem would miraculously go away and I would be fine. Because she had been so careful and focused in her examination, I honestly don't think it occurred to me that my optometrist might simply be wrong, or if I did, this alone I attributed to wishful thinking. I kept telling myself that many, many old people have this condition, and I wasn't in any way special, and so I should just shut up about it.

I consulted a friend who uses a white cane; I talked with an acquaintance with macular degeneration as well as other difficulties with her eyes. The first told me he could introduce me to the most wonderful people at the CNIB, praised them so highly I almost cancelled our lunch plans and went immediately to them. He promised me, too, that when the time came, he would show me the ropes of being legally blind. (In Alberta, legal blindness occurs if your best eye has less than 20/200 vision when corrected with glasses or contacts. 20/200 means "that a person cannot be more than 20 feet away to see what a person with normal vision can see from 200 feet away.")

The other acquaintance commiserated, not in an "oh, you poor thing" way, but more in a "damn it all! It's a helluva thing" way, which I liked, and offered me a high-resolution reading tool she no longer used. I noted, too, that though neither of them could see well enough to drive, they both went about the city with what seemed to me to be freedom, even insouciance, by using taxis and services for the disabled, and sometimes relying on friends or family. Is this perhaps doable after all, I asked myself? Finally, I bestirred myself enough to ask an ophthalmologist I knew if I should be taking some medicine or doing eye exercises or something to maybe ameliorate the progression of the condition. She told me to come and see her.

I got a referral. Convinced now that I had the disability and knowing that there was no cure, I had begun to try to be cheerful about my fate, or at least to try to find a livable, decent approach to it. A part of me was holding off, though. I could feel it; it was saying *wait, hold on*, the diagnosis isn't certain yet, you need to wait. In the soulful blackness of my interior, where I came to understandings and made firm decisions from which there would be no going back, I was still holding on, weightless, not daring to take too deep a breath. How I would handle blindness would have to come when I knew for sure that would be my fate.

Eventually, I told my friends. The people I knew who were legally blind, having lived in Calgary all their lives, had networks of friends, or close family members nearby, or both. I had friends, mostly younger than I am and there-fore busy already, who didn't need another drain on their energy; and anyway, I hadn't known them for more than five years. I knew they couldn't hand over their lives to me, and I would have been ashamed if I had caught one of them trying to. The possibility of moving closer to my son and his family I quashed at once: at least I knew my way intimately around my own condo, my building, and my neighbourhood. My sisters would not only be unable to help me — one was in a wheelchair and the other in serious ill health — but even with malfunctioning sight, I would still be the healthy one. At our ages, we wondered who would be the first to depart. It would be crazy to uproot myself at this moment in my life only to find myself, sooner rather than later, a stranger in a strange community, and blind.

Wait a minute, I told myself: you're jumping the gun; maybe your eyes are okay, and all this emotional turmoil is for nothing. Hah! I said to myself, with my history of bad luck? Quit kidding yourself; of course you're going blind, and do not ever forget that so are thousands of other old people. Blindness is commonplace as people grow old and then older again. And older after that. (A 2012 WHO report stated that in 2010, eighty-two percent of those blind and sixty-five percent of those with moderate and severe blindness were older than fifty.)

Such a diagnosis would be the end of people telling me how young I look for my years, which was a source of faintly surprised pride, I realized, no matter how much I pretended it wasn't, but that seemed hardly worth thinking about. When you're old, you're old; no matter what you look like, you are still in the last few years of your life: the last quarter, the last third, the last tenth. There may be a few advantages to looking younger than your age — the occasional younger male hits on you — there are also disadvantages: the same younger male vanishes when he finds out you are twelve or fifteen years older than he is, if not older than that. I lost one boyfriend because I was four years older than he was. I guess he thought that by the time I was eighty-four and in total swamp-creature decrepitude, he would still be eighty and continuing to make out with fifty-year-olds. As an adult woman in our age-hating society, the younger you look, the less likely you'll be ignored and/or dismissed, which is an important advantage, but no guarantee of anything else.

The day of my ophthalmologist's appointment arrived. After about forty-five minutes of sitting in front of one machine and then another, blinking or not-blinking as requested, my vision blurry from drops, she told me that I did not have macular degeneration. Then she told me that I had preconditions for glaucoma, which would require observation and, possibly, in a year or two, actual treatment. She was going to refer me to a retina specialist because she felt I was in steady danger of having detached retinas. "Oh," I said. I couldn't think of anything else to say. My entire brain had scrunched itself up into a puzzled, partially disbelieving — or maybe awed — frown.

The problems that had taken me to the optometrist in the first place were negligible and probably even fixable with a laser treatment or two. No thank you, I said. Better to let sleeping dogs lie, which, come to think of it, is what I say to my dentist, too, while crossing my fingers. (It's amazing to me how much I count on being dead before the real horrors get the chance to hit.) I saw that it was a good thing the optometrist had made a mistake, because without her diagnosis, I would never have seen the ophthalmologist, which turned out to be, if for different reasons, crucial for my continuing ability to see. At first friends said, "Thank heavens," when I said I didn't have macular degeneration, but I pointed out, "Medicine can slow glaucoma, but the condition can make you completely blind." Completely blind: without perceptible light. "While there is no treatment for macular degeneration, at least you aren't in full darkness." Despite everything, there was some room for relief, or joy. I just don't see very well, to go along with not hearing very well or sleeping very well, and with having achy joints, and occasional memory glitches. Ah, well, I thought finally, drawing in my breath shakily, surrendering to the inevitable finally getting its claws into me.

The hardest lesson of growing old is to recognize finally that you aren't special, that fate will do with you whatever it wants, just as it does with everybody on this planet. First, even though I didn't look or act old at all, fate made me old. Now, I, too — wonderful me! — could go legally blind like anybody else, and have to end my life using special aids, hiring people to assist me (if I could afford it) and spending most of my time alone in my condo listening to podcasts or whatever. Nothing special about that end; commonplace in our society, though no less a tragedy. Aging Gloucester, savagely blinded by his enemies. Blind Homer, telling one of the greatest tales ever told, that has lasted in written form for nearly three thousand years. Nor would I be dragging around the streets in rags, with my gnarled cane and my begging cup.

If you're lucky, as I am, you will get old incrementally, your body wearing out bit by tiny bit, small wound by small wound, your soul wearing away with it all, thinning, loosening from its anchors, eternity coming closer every day.

LETTUCE
Or Things I Can't Do Now That I'm Old

1. **MENTAL ARITHMETIC**: That's what calculators are for, but it feels kind of shameful that I can no longer do simple math in my head when I'm standing in front of the lettuce at the Co-op and try to figure out which is the better buy, given that I never manage to eat a whole package of torn lettuce before it starts to rot, never mind the same thing happening with all the other vegetables I buy to put in the salad. So, is the better buy to go over to the salad wagon, which is certainly the most expensive route, and make myself a ready-made salad that will last me maybe as much as three meals and nothing gets thrown out? What is the answer to $3.89 minus $2.44? I have no clue. I have to see it written down. Or, if my niece was born in 1972, how old is she now in ... whatever bloody year it is now — oh, 2020. I don't know, less than one hundred, more than fifteen.

2. READ HENRY JAMES: I find now that one of Henry James's very long and complex sentences semi-baffles me. While I can get the general meaning of the sentence as well as I ever did, the subtleties (wherein lie so much of the beauty and mystery for which James is famous — or used to be), elude me, especially if I'm tired or distracted. Imagine that I used to lose myself in Henry James; I used to be baffled by those who found him dull or who thought he was plain . . . obese . . . overt . . . wordy — what the heck is the word I'm trying to find?

3. AND THAT'S ANOTHER ONE: I cannot think of words, simple words, hard words, long ones, short ones, middle-of the road ones. I know they're there; I know if I have the patience — a day, two days, a week — the word will come to me. But I want it now: oh, I know, verbose. And yet, even that doesn't sound right. "Prolix," ghastly," "loquacious?" That one sounds so far off the track, and yet, I suppose the root is "lo . . ." something having to do with words — I never studied the roots of words in college; maybe the problem is just that loquacious is too fancy for what I'm trying to say. Maybe there is no such word as the one I'm struggling for. And yet, I can feel it out there, I can almost see it, wafting around in the delicate breeze, fluttering itself at me tauntingly, hazy, whitish, against a background of the palest blue, and yet I cannot bring it into focus. Sigh. So, verbose it will have to be.

4. MEMORY: So, I was washing the lettuce because I'm having guests for dinner tonight, and I was thinking about Henry James. Then I started thinking about the verbose/loquacious/ prolix thing, and I went to my books, where I found one on

the roots of English that I have owned for thirty years but —
I would have said, "never used," but there is a marker in the
K section and what on earth could I have been looking for
there? — and discovered the root of loquacious is loqui (Latin),
but the heading for it is "Tolkw," does that mean Tolkien?
How do I find out? Oh, but wait, I can hear the water running
in the kitchen. I guess I forgot to turn off the tap when I went
to look up — whatever it was I went to look up. Just a minute:
Didn't my guests say they would bring the salad? How do I
find out without being rude? Maybe I should make one just
in case, or am I thinking of some other time? Am I actually
absolutely sure this is the night they're coming? The other
day I saved containers of water and didn't flush the toilet all
morning because plumbers were coming to do an annual
reaming out of pipes or something, and it turned out I had
the wrong day, so that I went without water all morning and
into the early afternoon *twice*. (But told nobody because it is
hard enough for a visibly old guy to get any respect *without*
admitting to any actual mistakes, which only gets the younger
ones nodding meaningfully behind your back while mouthing to each other *"dementia."*)

5. **ABOUT THOSE CALCULATORS:** I don't carry one. Are you kidding?
Besides my feet, my left shoulder (sometimes it's my right), my
knees, and occasionally my lower back cause me so much
trouble that I can't carry heavy purses anymore. Everything
not absolutely required goes out of my purse before I embark
on my daily adventure, which is leaving my condo for any
reason whatsoever. Whether driving, walking, or taking the
bus. When I have reached the point where I can wake up in

the morning with a swollen ankle — how the hell can you sprain an ankle when you're sleeping? — I am not going to be carrying anything but my keys and my cellphone in case I fall and can't get up, or some jerk mugs me. I don't carry coins; they weigh too much. Too bad, because they could work like brass knuckles — also too heavy to carry.

6. SPELLING: I used to be the world's best speller, as was everybody else I know — my women friends, I mean — and now I can't trust myself to spell correctly the very words I used to be such a whiz at. It used to be "ei/ie" words came to me naturally, or maybe supernaturally, because I just *knew* how to spell them. Now I can't remember how to spell "niece" or "Keith" — not long ago I had to stop communicating with a friend with that name: it was just too embarrassing. Now I rely on spellchecker, which thirty years ago I totally scorned. I can't remember if we had spellchecker thirty years ago. But I do remember an hour's struggle recently over how to spell the word that means "entirely" or "totally." ("Wholly" was what I was looking for. I mean, I couldn't even think how to spell that initial sound! There was just a blank space in my brain where the way to write that sound should have been, or else a black hole sucking spelling into its maw forever.) Even now the word looks weird to me; or is it w - ie - rd? Should I even be writing anymore?

7. I FORGET THE OTHERS. A list of "Things I *Can* Do Now That I'm Old" to follow.

INGLORIOUS ON THE LRT

We were seated at the front of the first car on what seemed the oldest train in Calgary's Light Rail Transit fleet. We could see the driver's back, shadowy, cut by reflections, through the glass door in front of us, when the train stopped at a station, the doors slid open, and a short, thin man of maybe thirty years, dressed in a hoodie and rumpled pants, got on. Or rather, he slid in, staggering at the same time, grabbed a pole, and swung himself the rest of the way in, like a wobbly slow-motion version of Gene Kelly and the lamppost in "Singing in the Rain."

Safely inside, he bent from the waist and began grimacing, holding his forearm a few inches away from his abdomen like a mime pretending to rub his stomach but never actually touching it. He swung slowly around the pole until he reached the bench across from me, where, turning about, dog-like, several times, he curled into a fetal position, and continued to make agonized faces and mime clutching his stomach. Had he been beaten up? Was he sick? Drunk, on drugs, mentally ill? Should we push the emergency button? Dial 911? Move to the other end of the car?

But by the next stop, he was standing again, holding a pole, and had stopped the stomach-clutching and face-making. When the doors opened, he leaned out from the waist, flat-backed, as if his upper body was independent of his lower half, which he kept stiffly in place, knees locked. Great, we thought, he's getting off. But just as the doors were to close, his lower half pulled his upper half back into the car. At every subsequent stop, he repeated this manoeuvre. In between stations, he rolled around or sat on the floor or dragged himself up to swing in a circle from the pole in the same slow motion, sliding either up or down it, and, in between, letting go of the pole and staggering a few steps, during which, more than once, he banged inadvertently against the driver's door.

This caused the driver to stop the train and lean out, gazing inquiringly around the car, immediately spotting the offender, who managed to pull himself almost upright, manufacture a wavering grin at the driver, and give him a jaunty, Charlie-Chaplin tip of the nonexistent hat. Satisfied that we other passengers (most of whom had retreated to the back of the car) were not in danger, the driver, a turbaned Sikh at least a third bigger than the offender, went back into his cubicle and drove us on.

Even though I think the man was also drunk, on drugs, or both, much of what I was seeing seemed pure performance, and he was lost in it, not even once making eye contact with anyone, and, as I watched, I wondered what picture of himself he was seeing in his head — some cartoon character? — and what idea he was acting out. Like everybody else, at my downtown stop, rather than using the exit near him, I went to the doors at the car's other end and walked up the outside of the car, dodging disembarking passengers, keeping my eye on the exit where he was, as before, leaning unsteadily from the waist out the door. Using his pole to steady himself, he walked his feet ahead of his upper body, and bit by bit took both sections off the train, whereupon I lost sight of him in the crowd.

"You don't know what you're missing!" I said to the friends I was meeting, and they snorted, half-laughing, not getting that I was, more or less, serious, even though I admit that the things that happen on public transport aren't always that mystifying, or that interesting.

I take the train because I'm afraid of driving in stop-and-go traffic at my age, because the longer I have to do it (once for thirty-eight minutes to go two blocks), where a second's inattention means a fender-bender, the harder I find maintaining the necessary level of alertness. Worse, though, is driving on freeways at 100 kilometres or better, merging and changing lanes, drivers cutting you off, and massive, load-bearing trucks roaring past and around you, and where chances are that somebody drunk or high or suicidal — or just plain incompetent — is driving next to you. I'd rather take my car, but I know I haven't got what it takes anymore, and so, despite the worried expressions on my friends' faces, I take my chances on the buses and trains.

They think public transportation is dangerous, and I shouldn't use it, but I can only think that in the face of Calgary traffic, that's a joke. During the five years from 2008 to 2012 (according to the Statistical Report of the Calgary Police Service), a total of 143 traffic fatalities occurred on Calgary roads, while there have been only four homicides on transit property in 108 years (to summer 2017), and all of them since 2007, not to mention that all of them occurred not in the vehicles, but on the platforms, one caused by a woman pushing a seventeen-year-old to his death under a train. A horrific event, but with many thousands of transit-users on any given day still an extremely rare one, unlike traffic deaths on freeways and even on neighbourhood street corners.

More likely than being killed on a train or bus in Calgary is that you will be mightily annoyed, if not frightened, humiliated, disgusted — made supremely uncomfortable — by what happens there, I would say in particular on the LRT, probably because the driver is the only staff on board, and he is locked in his compartment with his back to his passengers. Still, most transit rides are merely boring, although, just as often as you're irritated, you will be touched, heartened or amused.

Once, when I had recently arrived in Calgary, I was heading home about 9:30 p.m. after an early movie with friends, when I heard my train coming. I started to run, not keen to stand on the platform alone at that hour, and managed to slip through the last door of the last car. I was pleased with myself, a country girl managing the city with aplomb. Until I looked up, then down the car. (This was one of those occasions when the seats all faced me, so that the passengers were riding backwards to their destinations.) I saw that all the seats of the front half of the car were occupied by heavily built, leather jacket–wearing, tattooed young men. They were grinning at each other, and making little faces of an aren't-we-clever variety, along with look-at-the-surprised-old-white-lady smirks.

My immediate reaction, after surprise, was a secret enjoyment bordering on pure delight, as if for once the universe and I were in sync. I only realized that it hadn't occurred to me to be afraid when at the next stop, a tall, too-thin white girl in her early twenties, nondescript in dark jacket and pants, got on the car, and, seeing the men, simply froze. But she was too late to get off again, the doors had closed, and although the seats at our end of the car were all empty, she stood, until, after a second, she unfroze, and turned her back to face the blank end wall of the train, as if, if she couldn't see them, they couldn't see her. Or perhaps she knew who they were, and unconsciously gestured to say, *I didn't see you.*

During all of this, not one of the men moved, and if one spoke, it was in an undertone that only the man sitting next to the speaker would have heard. I noted how their bodies were completely relaxed — were they maybe going to a party? — their expressions amused and self-congratulatory. When I finally got off the train, I might have rolled around in the snow, if I were forty years younger, with laughter at the fascinating sights the universe occasionally cooks up. After leaving the train, I got into my car and drove home, wondering all the while what those men, who in any other context would be very scary indeed, were up to, and was endlessly pleased because I'd seen them, astonishingly, unbelievably, riding the LRT.

I couldn't stop speculating about them. I thought of how at that time of night driving from one end of the city to the other would have been easy, so why take the train? Had they no self-respect? Maybe they were evading police, I thought, or rival gangs, possibly going to a meeting somewhere in the city's far south: What a coup! Not remotely badass, and brilliant because of that!

I suppose I should have been scared, but as I keep telling my friends, you don't have to worry about the street people, the people on drugs, the unmedicated schizophrenics, the toughs whether male or female: they only bother each other; they don't bother little old ladies, thinking them not worth the trouble, or maybe as with most of society, not even seeing them. Anyway, the police keep a very close eye on those downtown platforms. When I express this opinion to my friends, they tend to purse their lips and look away.

My firm impression is that the city's elites don't use public transportation, presumably because they would find themselves within coughing, spitting, and touching distance of The Great Unwashed; that is, me, although I don't see myself as belonging to "the underclass." I'm not poor, English is my first language, I don't wear conspicuous items of any religious or cultural groups, although if I were still a child and my father took the train to work, though white, he would have been of that class. In fact, now that I have largely given up the stress of driving in favour of public transportation, in my experience, during non-commuter hours, and given that twenty-eight percent of the city's population is now visible minorities, LRT riders are almost all people of colour and of different ethnicities. Often, I've noted, mine is the only white face in the car. I am moved by that observation, and I struggle to understand it. I assume my fellow transit users are mostly without cars (of course, lots of them are students), which would make them working class, and I wonder why none of them are white. I read somewhere an opinion that bringing in so many immigrants creates an underclass of visible minorities, which is an appalling thought to any social democrat or humanist, but not one I have any idea how to prevent or solve. Poor people, I am reminded, don't own cars.

Of course, I don't take the train after about 10:00 p.m., except for one night after the opera, when everybody on board the packed car was at least middle class, and a group of well-dressed young students stood together, and, with the best of good humour, sang popular songs all the way downtown, everybody in the car grinning with them, except for one sixtyish male opera-goer who, by his expressions and the worried glances his wife surreptitiously slid at him, appeared to find their behaviour, at the very least, disgraceful. The kids, happily, kept on singing lustily in the face of his furious disapproval.

On another night, my friend and I left the Calgary Stampede grounds after midnight. The platforms were packed, the trains crammed, there were even men there, as in Tokyo, to show people where there was still room on board. As we made our way down the packed car they had put us on, two young men began to stand, one saying to the other, "Let's give them our seats," and the other answering, "Yeah, they're fragile." We were glad to accept the seats, but tried not to laugh, because they seemed to us so young and vulnerable, and by comparison, we thought of ourselves as tough old babes. But I'm not forgetting the teenaged white girl sleeping alone well after midnight in the station close to my condo, who was raped there by two losers, or the Asian-Canadian woman who rode the train home from work at 2:00 a.m. and was followed and raped.

When I first arrived in Calgary, I began to note that, on public transit, too often for my taste, things go wrong: stations closed for upkeep, trains late or not running or that break down, the system that broadcasts station names out of sync with the stations, so that if you don't know by sight where you are, and the platform signs are blocked from your view, and you don't hear "next stop is . . .", you will get off at the wrong station. Of course, the worst is when somebody gets on the train drunk, high on drugs, or off his meds, or just plain looking for trouble, most of whom, although not all, as far as I've experienced, I'm sorry to say, are young men.

I once rode downtown in a full car, harangued all the way by a boy I guessed to be about twenty, apparently drunk, or at least drunk enough not to weigh the possible cost of his behaviour. I used to work in special education and as an educational psychologist, and I immediately thought that this kid was massively troubled, the kind of child to whom middle-class parents finally give a couple of thousand dollars and tell just to go away. He announced to us all that he was from Toronto, and that Calgary was hugely inferior to Toronto, not knowing that such a claim to Calgarians was simply risible, or that he himself was unwitting proof of the error of his claim.

I can't remember his silly insults that made you want to smack him, or boot him, depending if you were male or female. If, in response to his taunting, anybody so much as looked his way, he would fasten on that person and proceed to insult him or her. So after one or two had done so, and had been the object of the kid's brutal witlessness, nobody else looked at him, or responded to him in any way. It was the only time I've ever been in a full LRT car that was completely silent, where no one even moved.

But at the front of the car, a well-built man of about thirty-five leaned against the end wall. He was wearing a faded, lilac-coloured T-shirt with his worn jeans, and was clearly restraining himself with effort, shifting his position, rolling his head, his mouth occasionally moving. The kid taunted him as, "Purple T-shirt! Look at him! He wants to get his hands on me!" and the man barely containing himself, even though he, the kid, and everybody else knew he could make mincemeat of that skinny white boy.

In that silence we could all hear the kid's seat companion muttering to him, "You better get off. The police will be waiting at the next station." I could see him hesitating, trying to decide if he would tough it out or not, and at the last second chickening out. Purple T-shirt stepped off the train there too, but, changing his mind before the doors closed, got back on. I suppose the whole car might have risen up, dragged the kid out of his seat, and thrown him off the train, but knowing this aggravation wouldn't last more than another ten minutes or so, and that for all his mouthiness he wasn't physically dangerous, people saw this as just another day on the LRT. On such days, probably like everybody else, I wondered if maybe I could manage driving my car downtown, find a place to park that wouldn't cost the earth, give up being self-righteously environmentally conscious (one of the reasons I give my friends for taking public transit).

Or, on an especially frigid Sunday morning, the kind of day when many people abandon their plans and stay home, and a few of the more intrepid take the train instead of their cars, I was heading downtown for lunch and a matinee with friends. Three Indigenous women who could have been in their forties got on the train and sat down, two of them across from me and one beside me. Every other person in the car promptly got up and moved to the next car, at which there was zero reaction from the women, as if this always happened and wasn't worth noting, leaving me alone with them. The woman who had plunked herself partially on me moved an inch or two to get level seating, which, I am sure, was all she noticed, that there was a lump under her, and she needed to move off it, although she succeeded only partially. They began to talk together in soft voices, their faces still, non-expressive, their sentences short and mostly unfinished, just the operative part, no pointless chitter-chatter as white women would have gotten into. Even their laughter was brief and soft.

The conversation, punctuated by long silences, was about meeting friends downtown and spending the day in this or that bar with whomever they expected to run into. I sat perfectly still; my liberal conscience and my supportiveness for the cause of justice for the First Nations people of the plains would absolutely not allow me to move out of the car, and they seemed not in the least dangerous, and I would be damned if I would do such a racist thing. How many times had I been in a car with semi-drunk young white kids, and a couple of times with falling-down drunks, and never given it a thought? And so I sat, hardly breathing, enfolded in my thick down-filled coat, my toque, wool scarf, my fur-lined mitts, my boots. They had apparently forgotten I was there, or at least the woman pressed up against me had. Once, volunteering at a Healing Lodge — a facility for federally sentenced Aboriginal women — I watched a woman who had already been in a regular prison for a dozen years, and who didn't want to be noticed by the prison officer speaking to me, pull in *something* I hadn't known was part of a human being, to almost disappear. Thus, I know that it is possible for people who wish not to be noticed to pull in some aura or something humans normally radiate, so that other people hardly register you're there. I think I must have been unconsciously doing that, and that was why my presence seemed to have been forgotten by the other women.

At the next stop, a middle-aged, middle-sized white woman got on and sat across and down from me next to the two Indigenous women, which none of the other travellers had done, choosing instead to go into the next car. It seemed to me that she was on her way to church, perhaps because she was carrying what seemed to be a bible or a hymnal. She spoke to the women sitting across from me and to the woman beside me, a normal conversation, none of which I can remember: the awful cold of the day, for one thing. I think I had drifted off a bit, wasn't focusing on them anymore. Again, none of them seemed to have noticed or remembered that I was there.

During this Chekhovian vignette, the white woman, looking faintly taken aback and after hesitating fractionally, was taking off her colourful knitted wool mitts, and mutely handed them across the aisle to the woman who was sitting squeezed up against and partially on me. I realized that the Indigenous woman had asked for them. (Had the white woman asked her where her mitts were, or remarked that it was too cold to be out without mitts, and so the Indigenous woman asked the white woman for hers?) It was clear that, although she was taken aback by the request, the white woman's well-trained but probably unchallenged-to-this-minute Christian self would not allow her to refuse. I don't think the Indigenous woman put on the mitts, she just kept them on her lap. During this interchange, her two companions didn't move, or speak, or show any emotion.

A minute or two more of silence, the Indigenous woman said something I couldn't hear, even though she couldn't have been closer to me, and the white woman was taking off her matching scarf and handing it mutely across the aisle to the Indigenous woman, who accepted it without a word. The white woman was crying now. At the next stop, she got off, sans scarf or mitts, still silently crying. I watched her hurry to the platform exit and disappear down the stairs while the train moved on. The Indigenous woman watched her impassively, too, while her friends, equally impassively, watched their friend. No one spoke or moved.

The next stop was mine, so I extracted myself from semi-under the Indigenous woman — it was all these bulky clothes we were wearing, and also my absolute silence and motionlessness, that caused her to not notice she was almost sitting on me — and stood up. When I inadvertently nudged her in pulling my coat out from under her, she snapped her head around to me — she really had forgotten I was there — and at last I saw emotion in her face: a spark of heightened alertness, instant, pure, perhaps that someone had witnessed her actions, or maybe she was merely startled at my sudden materialization. I met her eyes for an infinitesimal beat, just long enough to wonder if what I saw was fear; I walked the few feet between her and her two friends to the door and got off the train.

Had any of the three Indigenous women worn hats, scarves, or mitts? I remember only that they all had on boots and winter coats, although none looked as warm as mine. The other white woman's coat wasn't as warm as mine, either, but I have spent half my life in the countryside, where there is no rescue if you are ill-equipped, and I keep those self-protective rural habits even now, here, in the city. I wondered then, and I wonder now, if the one who had taken the scarf and mitts, when she got off the train, then, in disgust or rage or a flood of bitterness dropped them in the trash on the station platform, or if she wore them in triumph.

I wondered if she had been a victim of the Indian Residential School system (the last one was in Saskatchewan and closed in 1996, so it was possible), but in Canada, Indigenous people live with systemic racism. Even the rock-bottom layer of virulent hatred of and disgust at the very condition of being Indigenous still exists in places, and would scare the wits out of you if you if you actually saw it, but is well hidden from decent non-Indigenous people and experienced only by the Indigenous. I find that hatred to be bloody well subhuman. I try, but I make no claims about my own righteousness; it's faulty, sometimes absent, always strained, usually helpless. After all, I just sat there and watched and listened and didn't move a muscle or speak, so the fact that I was there would be forgotten, although, what would I have said? What might I have done? And so I report the incident and my inglorious non-part in it here. If nothing else, though, the incident illustrates how difficult and conflicted our relations still are, no matter how decent we try to be (or think we are being), or how beautifully we speak about our equality as Canadians.

Days later, I wondered what the Indigenous woman would have done if the white woman, seeing she had no mitts or scarf, had simply taken hers off and given them in a firm but straightforward way to the Indigenous woman. Would the Indigenous woman have indignantly refused them? The power balance then would have shifted, but I cannot fully grasp the possibilities.

Generally, though, I often think it deplorably strange that I am almost never in a group of Calgarians with anybody of colour and/or non-Christian, non-European in origin, and awful as I know it sounds, almost the only time I am around racialized people is when I take public transport. I am dismayed by how narrow a world I live in. I have the excuse of my advanced age, which makes it hard to strike out in new directions (frankly, makes it hard to do anything), my timid personality, and my laziness. The truth is, the older I get, the more my world narrows. But riding the buses and the LRT, I get to feel I am still part of life, not just the white, Christian, middle-class life, always taking the easy way out, marking the same well-trodden paths, never thinking beyond the world I was born into and raised in. (The one I was born into in north-central Saskatchewan was Indigenous/white and that was about it. And it was so long ago that only the Indigenous men who worked, sometimes, for my father in his sawmill, spoke English; their wives and children, living in their tipis in the field behind our log house, apparently didn't.) I'm aware, though, that my fellow train riders would find me, at the least, condescending.

But skin colour is hardly the only issue; a glimpse of other ways of living is also part of what I have lost, and I think that people who never use public transportation (because they don't have to) are ignorant of the real life of their own city. I suppose they would say, if anyone asked, that they were well aware of the large population who use the transit system outside of commuter hours, those who are poor, and often, in my experience, *mostly* of colour, and that they already knew all they needed to know about their lives — such a distant, uninvolved knowledge, guaranteed not to stir the heart or challenge their beliefs.

Public transportation struggles mightily to get more riders, for reasons from paying for this service itself so vital to those who have no choice, to the undeniable environmental benefits: private cars choking the roads are terrible for the environment as everybody knows. But it has to overcome the snob factor, first: I'm too good to ride the bus or be crowded into a packed LRT car; then the racist factor: people who are not like me take the bus; and also, as I mentioned above, the perceived-danger factor: public transportation isn't safe, presumably because criminals take public transport? I can't think what else it's not safe from. But, somewhere in there is also the nuisance factor: all kinds of people from the non-medicated mentally ill to the annoying, too-loud young will be found on buses and trains.

One morning fairly early, I was on a bus heading to my local LRT station when a young, exhausted-looking man in work clothes got on and began talking with the driver (forbidden, of course, but there was nobody else on the bus). He explained to the driver, whom he seemed to know, that he had had to quit his job out at such-and-such company (at the very edge of the city), because the city had stopped bus service there, and he didn't have a car. He had managed to find work closer to his home, but it didn't pay as well, and in other ways wasn't as good a job, a perfect illustration of how vital affordable, well-mapped, and egalitarian public transportation is.

As far as visible minorities are concerned, though, public transportation has always been a fraught subject, especially in the American south and in the sprawling megalopolis of Los Angeles where large numbers of people of colour tend to be concentrated in particular areas.

According to *Bloomberg*, in 2012, ninety-two percent of LA bus riders were people of colour, and in 1995, sixty-nine percent of US bus riders were. I know that, historically, in some American states, provision of affordable public transportation has been used by city councils as a weapon against African-American, Hispanic, and other non-white minorities by giving them substandard services and/or denying them services to the places where the jobs are, effectively keeping them poor and unintegrated. A few years ago, even Toronto had a brouhaha, brought to a head during a municipal election, over public transportation proposals that would have skipped service to a couple of areas where visible minorities are concentrated. I haven't heard of any such complaints in Calgary, a city of about 1.3 million (much smaller than

Toronto's 2.8, while the Greater Toronto Area is home to around 4.7 million), and it seems that in Calgary, visible minorities are present throughout the city rather than, for the most part, clustered in any one area. And yet, why was I often one of the few if not the only white person in an LRT car (when it wasn't commuter hours)? Maybe the concentration of visible minorities on the trains will change when all seven of the more convenient and faster (than regular buses) MAX (Bus Rapid Transit) buses (estimated costs in total just over one hundred million dollars) are all up and running, at least one of them specifically intended for an underserved area.

A main provision for public transportation is, of course, roads, an expensive mode of transporting people used mostly by the owners of private vehicles. Prior to my ridership on buses and trains, when out with a friend in the far north-west of Calgary, I saw the network of new freeways being built, and, thinking of the cost — at which I can only guess — and the masses of gas-guzzling, environment-polluting cars they would encourage, I was stunned and then angry. To the south, passage has nearly come to a halt with all the new road construction. This is madness, I thought; this is what is ending our world. And, as someone said to me the other day, if the city didn't keep approving new subdivisions, there wouldn't be any need for the roads.

Then there are the in-city train lines such as the LRT I ride. Calgary's first LRT line went into the northwest corner of the city, where people are, relatively speaking, middle to upper middle class. (The University of Calgary, with its student population of around thirty-two thousand, is there, and was probably an important factor in deciding where to start the

LRT line.) But the massive new LRT Green Line will go from the north centre part of the city to the far southern edge of the city, with twenty-eight new stations: forty-six kilometres of new track will cost enough to make the jaw drop, compared especially to the cost of the MAX bus services. The first section to be built alone is estimated at costing nearly five billion dollars. Yet, buses are the cheapest form of public transportation and can penetrate areas where other kinds of services can't. Recently, though, when the Calgary city council wanted to save money, it cut LRT and bus services, even eliminating a couple of bus lines, and, in my opinion, worst of all, cutting back on transportation services for the disabled. Without services, it is the poor and lower middle class, those who may well not own cars or who can't afford to drive them every day, or to pay for parking, who suffer the most.

But I ride transit regularly all over the city among them, as an equal in the sense of also feeling (as I am sure many of them do) that one has no other real choice. And so, I'm witness, through careful although hidden scrutiny, to the occasional brief conversation or shared smile over a child or a difficulty, or an exchange of commiseration over some happening, sometimes riders asking for help about stops or bus numbers to reach a certain destination, or to the vignettes and the nasty occurrences I have mentioned above.

Your transit-riding fellow citizens might even be in the majority over the car-drivers: the young man in plaster-dusted coveralls, carrying a lunchbox and unsteady with fatigue, who announces to the car that he is taking a seat, "because I been on my feet for twelve hours," and nobody protests or comments, or the hijab-and-robe-wearing young woman who says in halting English, because you spoke a little to her, "You are a good person," (like hell you are), and you suspect she is riding the train from end to end simply to keep from going mad from loneliness in this new country, or the man of colour, younger than you, who tells you not to sit on the seat you were planning to because the man sitting beside it, whom you didn't notice, is very drunk and will fall over on you when the driver brakes, and squeezes over to make room for you beside him, or the blonde six-year-old with a pretty design painted on her delicate little face, who has been to some event with her young father, who, after a brief chat, says softly to you, as she gazes into space, in a tone that breaks your heart, "Maybe the three of us could get on the train again, and we could ride and talk to each other," and you reply as gently as you know how to, because you understand or suspect there is no mother here, and not enough of that motherly love from the father, "It could happen, yes. Wouldn't that be great?" And then you cannot ever forget her.

SHARON DEALS WITH THE PROBLEM OF EVIL

A few nights ago, I woke up at about three in the morning and couldn't go back to sleep. February had been very cold for close to three weeks, during which I'd been mostly stuck alone in my condo trying to entertain myself and to hold off self-pity, which had begun to loom large. When I woke on the night in question, I found myself in a very deep, very dark space, probably the darkest I've ever been in as an older adult. I wasn't suffering from depression or any other particular affect caused by a death or a betrayal, for example, which would have been the source of such a state when I was a young adult. I was simply awake in the middle of a continuing, further consideration of my own ideas about the world and why we are alive on earth and where we are going at death.

Bit by bit, day after day, I paced, alone in my condo while outside the snow continued to fall, the temperature descended further, and sometimes the wind stormed and howled. Events were cancelled to which I wouldn't have been able to get anyway, and the phone did not ring, so I thought and read and thought. During this period, slowly drifting away from me had been anticipation of any future happiness for me on earth (or even entertainment or interest in daily occurrences), what usually occupies the background of our days and nights. As they slowly melted away, my thinking on these serious questions about who we are, where we come from, and where we're going had moved to the forefront of my mind.

Although I have been thinking about these things off and on for the last forty years, a passage I had read the day before in Yuval Noah Harari's *Sapiens: A Brief History of Humankind* caused me pause: "So monotheism explains order, but is mystified by evil. Dualism explains evil, but is puzzled by order. There is one logical way of solving the riddle: to argue that there is a single omnipotent God who created the entire universe — and He's evil. But nobody in history had the stomach for such a belief."

Given that I can't bring myself to believe in God, and lean perhaps toward Gnosticism, because clearly there is evil — I believe, incarnate — on earth, perhaps I should consider Harari's third category: that evil rules, and good, though present too, is subordinate. I tried to imagine a world in which evil rules in everyday life and thought that, as far as I could see — the view from the ground and not from theological or philosophical texts — there are two causes of bad happenings on earth, that is, those which cause suffering. (Pay attention now.)

Number one, I thought, has to be neurotic people, not those who are definably mentally ill and can be cured by drugs, or who can't be cured, but instead, those who by reason of, at some stage, having been mistreated or part of a terrible incident, and in the absence of wise counsel, support, good influences, and teaching, have suffered from that earlier mistreatment or accident, and, because of it, feel that now they have the right to happiness, even if it means taking it away from someone else. This narcissism might also feel furthered by hurting others even if only by shoving ahead in a line at the post office or snubbing someone for no reason, or saying mean things about someone behind her back, knowing that eventually that person will hear about it and suffer because of it.

I've often run into people who go through life tormenting others, not unusual at all, and if I had the stomach for it, which I don't, I could write pages about being victim in such incidents in my own life, the latest one only a couple of days ago. Even though trivial, that most recent incident was so egregious, and the perpetrator so self-righteous and so self-absorbed, so just plain ill-mannered, that my soul positively burned over it for a couple of days afterwards. I'm still rewriting the scenario in my head, what I should have said, what I should have done. Though insignificant in the degree of brutality — my life or physical well-being remained perfectly intact — the incident hurt me, I have suffered from it. While the guilty person didn't even notice how very bad her behaviour was, she felt perfectly entitled to do what she did, because in her mind her needs overrode my rights, because I wasn't as worthy a person as she was. In other words, she was someone who has gone and will go on through her life blindly leaving a trail of damage behind her. Confront such a person, and you will get only anger at your audacity, and complete denial.

I'd also been watching the television comedy *The Good Place*, the premise of which is that everybody wants to avoid eternal suffering in hell and to get to "the good place," otherwise known as heaven. The program is something new in the world of sitcoms, in that it is about how to be a good person, how not to continually torment other people with our blind assumptions, our carelessness, our selfishness and narcissism. One character, a professor of moral philosophy, instructs the other deceased characters on ideas of what constitutes good behaviour, and the writing is brilliant, and often very humorous. Until I watched the series, I thought that maybe I was the only person who actually noticed how insidious, omnipresent, and banal this kind of behaviour is, and how it contributes to our daily, mostly unearned misery on this earth.

The other cause of suffering on earth is that which allies with evil itself. I will be exact. Evil forces exist that magnetize humans so that they meld their own small evil to the larger sweep and force of evil in human history. What do you think happened in Rwanda? Mass hysteria, I suppose.

NOT LONG AGO, I came into the ken of one of these evil (presumably ancient) forces through the machinations of one very bad human dude who got his kicks out of allying himself with evil. Let's call him Mr. Evil. Rather than denying it, he shook all over like a maraca when confronted with one of his crimes, indicating to me that he knew he was in the wrong. His response puzzled me. Good people apologize, are contrite, and suffer badly from their errors; some may worry that the wrong they did will cause them to suffer in the afterlife. I never heard an apology from the bad guy, or any indication of anything other than what sure looked like fear, so I have to think he was worried about his fate in the afterlife. Or, perhaps, he was afraid not of having done wrong, but of having been caught, and potentially of punishment — maybe that was what he saw as his failing, and that failing was, for him, a very dangerous thing.

Of course, I was afraid of Mr. Evil, who seemed to me a disgusting excuse for a human being, afraid of the harm he knew how to mete out and his willingness to. I used to wonder what would become of him when he died — I was one of the very few, possibly one of only a couple, humans who saw him for what he was — and I thought that maybe he would be completely snuffed out on his death: gone forever from the universe of things, ideas, of history. That seemed to me an appropriate end for him, although also galling because it meant he would never suffer for his crimes, which were many, and some of which I am pretty sure were of the most heinous nature. If you're snuffed right out, you don't even know you're snuffed out, because you don't exist; there is no *you*. Would that victory of the good count on our way to eradicating all evil, step by miniscule step? Can goodness close the resulting gap or would another form of evil step right up to fill the vacuum?

In the night last night, I wondered if possibly Mr. Evil would instead, on death, join that entity he had audaciously (and probably in terror) aligned himself with in life, so that he would have the pleasure of carrying out his own despicable wishes without his victim in any particular case, for whom he was supposed to be a best friend or a mentor, knowing. He wanted to have power in the world; he wanted not to suffer, without amelioration or justice, from the torments all the rest of us suffer from every single day. He wanted power so badly he would be willing to ruin lives, to kill for it, to accept the fate of hell itself, if only he surrendered himself to the level of evil that presided over him and occasionally helped him.

Or, last night, I thought that perhaps Mr. Evil would align himself in death with that power I can't name, but that probably has a name as ancient as the world. I think Mr. Evil wanted to become a part of the greatest power, the power of evil, as sainted and angelic people long to align themselves with the greatest forces for good.

But, I thought, musing on because I had nothing to distract me, maybe Mr. Evil had been duped. He had chosen to align forces with, to become an instrument of the evil entity, albeit a more intimate and powerful instrument, with — possibly — the promise that he might one day join that entity, not be snuffed out, and instead, have huge power forever. But, I thought, what if instead on death he would not be saved; instead, he would be in for a big surprise. Although having been raised a Roman Catholic — just enough to learn my own kind of terror — I suddenly saw a reason for the legend of Hell, a place fit only for the likes of Mr. Evil. Surely he is not the only person willing to choose doing evil in order to have power in the world, while presenting himself to the world as completely normal, just another guy.

I wonder also what brought Mr. Evil to the point where he made the decision to align himself with evil. He must have known himself as a capable person, but one met on all sides by frustration and possibly abuse, and had decided to fight back in a way that wouldn't damage him and his life on a daily basis as would becoming a serial killer or a mass bank robber or rapist. Oh, no, he probably thought, I am meant for bigger things than that sort of squalid human activity. This way, he could be hugely powerful, but secretly, so he wouldn't suffer any consequences for his viciousness.

I think that the narcissism, selfishness, and lack of empathy and compassion, if too out of balance with saner, gentler human qualities, *can* open the way for real evil to creep in, even maybe to take over a particular human. Fortunately, most damaging neurotics aren't so audacious as the man I'm writing about, and they draw back from committing acts of real evil, and often feel regret, sorrow, and shame for any damage they might have done, often by just not noticing the needs of others, which is quite different from deliberately going out to do as much damage to others as possible.

Let's simplify and return to the notion of two entities, the force for good and the force for evil, which remain in an eternal struggle, but one where evil is the more powerful than good. How should I reconcile with that possibility? When I consider my own life and the lives of others I have known, and especially as I have aged, I see the suffering that rules most of the earth, always in service of the few who control all the wealth and earthly power and think the world exists only to serve them. Throughout my life I have watched dictators fall — Pol Pot, Nicolae Ceausescu, Muammar Gaddafi, Saddam Hussein, and saw that none of them, once caught, tried to run or fight or struggle as the noose approached, as the guns were raised against them, but instead seemed to know, always to have known, even as they killed, tortured, maimed, and starved a population and stole everything from their own people, that this ending was their fate. So does Mr. Evil appreciate that his end may well be unimaginably terrible? And yet, the gun, the knife, the forced suicide, is hardly justice. And torture? A monstrous foolishness and no true justice at all, and, I think, demeaning for the perpetrators more than for the victim.

I'm not convinced there is any way on earth to achieve justice against evil. There is only survival in the face of it, and as Manichaeans (a religion that began with Mani's teaching in the third century C.E., and that lasted in some countries as late as the fourteenth century C.E., so no meaningless blip, but a serious belief system) believed "salvation is obtained primarily through knowledge," of the kind we all begin struggling to find even when we are very young. "Knowledge" here refers to spiritual knowledge, and Mani says it begins with self-knowledge. I can't help but remember how many times during my later adult life I have watched people's eyes go blank, as if an invisible shield has come down over them, when they are confronted with their deliberate and deniable misdeed. Looking at those blank eyes, but aware of what has really happened, I realize that the perpetrator will make no admission, and I turn away in mild disgust, knowing I've met a person with willful blindness towards their own true nature.

And There Was Light is the autobiography of Jacques Lusseyran, who, at seventeen years old, and blind since childhood, was a leader of the French Resistance in Paris during the Second World War. One of his friends betrayed him to the Gestapo, and Lusseyran recounts in the book that critical moment when he should have recognized the approaching betrayal. Instead, a bar of blackness came over his inner vision, and he didn't or couldn't see the advent of evil. When I read this story, I realized that I had experienced something similar but much less crucial at the hands of Mr. Evil. As far as I can remember, he asked me a question, and I hesitated, not sure I should give him the information that would have been in my answer. I saw that black bar come down over — well, I don't exactly know what it came down over, but I think of it, or see it, as blanking out the warning not to reply. Instead of stopping, like an idiot, I panicked, denying the really weird black bar (or so frightened of it I just wanted to get whatever was going to happen over with), and I hurried on with what I had to say, when I'd have been much better to keep quiet, or else to say something very different. And then I had given away the information, and it was too late. After I read Lusseyran, I remembered this and vowed to stay alert so it would never happen to me again. The odd thing is that I *knew* the bar was something very bad when I caught a glimpse of it, but I was so frightened by it, and felt helpless against it, that I panicked and denied it was even there. Even thinking hard about it now, my blood rushes to my face, and I can feel my heart speeding up, before I force myself to calm down.

The dark thoughts that came to me in the middle of the night about our lives on earth remind me of my realization, perhaps twenty or more years ago, about how very evil the world really is. And nowhere, not at home, in church, in school, or in society in general was I taught to believe that evil prevails. Past mid-life, this realization was earthshattering, it made me stagger with horror and shock, it made me physically ill, to see that just below the surface that I was raised to believe in — with goodness and justice prevailing — was, in fact a squirming, putrid mass of cruelty and evil.

In my quest for knowledge after waking in the night, my thoughts had gone beyond that terror, the horror, the hopelessness caused by the knowledge of the evil just below the surface of "normal" life on earth. For the very first time in my life, I began to think that death with no subsequent consciousness at all, which due to my upbringing I'd always thought of as untrue, would be preferable to arriving at another, if somewhat elevated, bodiless realm or state where unknowable mysteries and torments would rain down on me.

And yet, even in the midst of evil, I feel being a force on the side of the good remains possible! We all know people, everyday people, friends, neighbours, relatives, who, as my grandmother and mother would have said, "haven't a mean bone in their bodies," and even though they haven't given their lives to one religion or another, just seem to constantly, no matter what, behave well. Throughout their lives, they mindfully do their best to avoid hurting others, and their quiet, steady presence is soothing to any troubled soul, and their kindness extends to animals and birds as well. Not being one of those people myself, I have always wondered how they do it, how they found the centre of themselves out of which it seems their decency comes.

I have for some years also believed in the presence of guardian spirits, what I was taught to call "guardian angels" when I was a child, although I don't think anyone actually believed in them then. Why should we have? None of us had the faintest presentiment of such a thing — just more pie-in-the-sky stuff, we must have thought, even as kids. I lived among poor children, children whose parents were uneducated, and some of whom were not attuned to child psychology, even a few who caused their own children more suffering than they saved them from. So, why should children in that situation believe they have a guardian angel when such an angel never saved them from anything they could see? And yet, even in those lives there was goodness: the parents' indubitable ties to their children, that they fed and clothed them and gave them beds to sleep in, children's own love for their siblings no matter how horribly they treated each other. And simple acts of goodness, so small the people doing them wouldn't even recognize them as such. Did we as children have a partly frightened, partly awed sense that their own private angel might exist, unseen, beside them? I remember my silent doubt at such a notion, that would eventually turn to contempt of it, and then, twenty or so years later, to a puzzled but awed belief. And, I must say, as I'm sure I'll be accused of childishness, that I don't think this is a childish belief — I didn't believe as a child — and that this is more likely a deeply mature belief. It is very hard, I acknowledge, for moderns to "give in" to what seems to be mere folklore and/or cant. Perhaps guardian angels are simply a conscience.

But they may save your life when they can, by whispering in your ear, as mine did when my car slid off an icy road toward a high embankment. "Now brake!" it said, and frozen in panic and fear at the wheel, I bestirred myself and braked, and stopped the car before it crashed into the bank at a too-high speed. Others have told me of similar instances in their own lives; in fact, I think there is a whole literature about such happenings. A friend told me about how as an adolescent she had been about to step down from the curb onto a busy street and felt a heavy hand on her shoulder pulling her back, just as a large truck roared around the corner and would have killed her. But when she looked around, there was no one there. She and the few others who have told me such stories marvel and wonder over them all their lives. I don't know what they conclude about their experiences of being saved from certain destruction other than that they felt the presence of someone they couldn't see, whose job seemed to be to rescue them from certain death, and whom they would, of course, define as good. And further — who wouldn't wonder — if they had been timestamped at birth, and their time hadn't yet come?

Although I haven't been able since my twenties to believe in a god, I have instead tried to understand life from and through my own experiences, staring as far into my own psyche and my own soul as I was able to go at the time, over more than fifty years. I haven't actively looked for God, as so many people do, but I have instead started at the bottom and looked for tiny little sources, pinpricks, of goodness and tried to figure out where they came from. I can just see all the theologians and philosophers groaning and wrinkling their noses over such utter naiveté; they would probably think, stupidity. And my reply? Let's keep it simple, okay?

I think that if there is an omnipotent distant God somewhere, He really has nothing to do with us poor rioting, killing, maiming, suffering creatures here on earth. I think that we must be less than worms crawling in mud to Him.

I think that if He exists, then after His creation of us, we are on our own. (Oh, oh — have I fallen into the doctrine of Free Will by accident?) This God-who-exists-but-doesn't-involve-Himself-in-the-affairs-of-humans is hardly the God of conventionally religious people — those whose ideas I cannot accept — and trying to sort out what I really think about a God, lately I've been wondering if maybe there might be one after all. I am quite shocked to find myself thinking this, and I do so because I have to admit that if I put my mind to the idea of the utmost, the very edge of the universe, I find what may or may not be there clothed so impenetrably in a final mystery as to what it consists of and how it got there that I think God must be the only, the ultimate cause. (Surely biology cannot account for these things.) I think, too, that those eternal questions cannot be answered on earth. But the Manichaeist belief in the need for self-knowledge tells us to go on deeper and deeper into the self, until this spark of God, instilled in all of us at creation, is found.

As I walk the prairie in solitude, day after day, as I have done for more than thirty years, thinking about myself as a human entity, a person, I retreat away from insanity-inducing thoughts about what exists beyond the edge of the universe. But this question was inspired in me, many years ago when I was a rancher's wife, by the sky on moonless nights, when there was no other source of light on the prairie but single farmyard lights many miles away. I would stare and stare upward, nearly falling to my knees with dizziness and wonder at what I saw. I would wonder what was in, or far, far beyond, those dark spaces between the vast panoply of stars, constellations, and galaxies that I saw with such clarity, too many to comprehend. A lifelong city dweller can barely imagine all that we could see on such nights when no moon shone. Shaken, I came back inside myself, down, down, down, until I found what I believed was the universal self, whether sparked by God or not. I tried to build a truth in answer to my questions that fit with what very little I knew, because I had seen it myself, and heard it, and felt it.

In the end, at nearly eighty, I try to find and practise humility, and more tolerance for other ideas. I am trying, bit by bit, to extract myself from all the things I always thought were life: romance, entanglement in the lives and dramas of others, involvement in the consumer culture, and ambition (I doubt I'll ever be able to kill that one completely); to recognize, dial down, and dissolve my own foolish desires. Some of this just happens; after nearly eighty years, you get tired of this whole business of being a human being on this earth, but some of it you have to think your way through to come out the other side. Ultimate questions — I think that was where I began — I haven't the brains for them, although I am constructing a tiny, personal spiritual view, and pathetically simple as it is, and I've no doubt quite inadequate to the philosophers of the world, it's what I have and will have to do.

But I have never forgotten my brilliant first husband, the love of my youth and father of my only child, saying that when he was a child he could never understand how when one person falls down, why everybody doesn't fall down. But that is another essay, and I would need another eighty years to figure that one out and write it.

THE MURDER REMAINS UNSOLVED

2021 marks fifty-nine years since beauty queen Alexandra Wiwcharuk was beaten, raped, and murdered, and her body buried in a shallow grave in a copse of trees near the weir on the northeast bank of the South Saskatchewan River in Saskatoon, Saskatchewan. A few weeks earlier, in April, she had turned twenty-three. She had already graduated from nursing school in Yorkton, Saskatchewan, and had been employed as a nurse at Saskatoon City Hospital since the previous September. Nobody doubted then, nor doubts now, that her killer was a man, not a woman, or possibly more than one man, that probably they were young, that she had refused them sexual favours, and that when they tried to force her, she fought back with all her strength and tried to escape, resulting in her smashed-in face, her skull broken in at the back, all her cranium's seams also broken, her rape, and then, after she was buried, her death by asphyxiation. A roughly thirteen-pound chunk of cement sat on her chest, suggesting her killer(s) knew she was still alive, but thought that the weight would keep her from getting up. They must have expected her to stop breathing very soon.

Such a terrible crime, the width and depth of its wickedness unheard of in our small city, and the more shocking because of the beauty and the decency of the dead young woman, the rarity of murders in Saskatoon at all, and the ensuing failure of the police to solve the crime. Now, today, as I write this, going over yet again all I know and all I don't know, I picture young men secretly called in and questioned in the police station, swearing they know nothing about it, proffering alibis, hinting, maybe, that somebody else might have been the guilty one(s). I try to imagine, too, as rumour has always had it, senior officers and maybe some from the city's hierarchy of "important" men, realizing who was guilty, and in consternation at the ringleader's identity, meeting clandestinely and deciding that the senior police officers should map out a secret plan to scuttle any real investigation while pretending to carry out a thorough one. This, in order to ensure the citizens never found out who that ringleader was. That has been the conjecture of a lot, if not most, of the people who were young in those days in Saskatoon (population then about one hundred thousand), and if you talk to them today — those still alive — this is what some will tell you they still suspect happened.

Although it took me years, I finally understood how commonplace it is, when a truly heinous crime is committed and the perpetrator isn't caught, that an explanation of this kind circulates throughout the general public; folklorists love to pursue the origins of such rumours. Years ago, did two stories get conflated? I know of such a case in Kansas, having talked with a historian who, through research in the city's archives, put the false story to rest. I also suspect that by then, maybe forty years after the event had happened, and since murder wasn't involved, the public persisted in believing the more interesting false story. But a lot of the time, and in Alex's case, in the absence of facts, people continue to suspect something corrupt must have gone on that explains why the killer(s) weren't caught.

What caused the rumour in Alex's case — that the police had identified the culprit, but were protecting a prominent person — was, as far as I can see, not much more than their continuing failure to catch the killer(s). Of course, in some cases, this explanation — protection of a prominent person — has turned out to be true, but nobody has ever made public any evidence that it happened this time, and despite the fact that suspicion continues to linger after nearly sixty years, the theory must remain just that, a rumour.

Besides this obvious mystery, two more remain to this day. The first is, did she have a single killer, or were there two or possibly three young men involved; and the second is, outside of the murder and police response to it, why is it that to this day, fifty-nine years later, instead of long ago forgetting it, Alex's story remains of unusual interest to the people of Saskatoon? The first I have finally resolved in my own mind:

I now think she had only one killer. The second, I tried to answer in a book I wrote about the case, an answer too long to write here. Later, I wrote a second book stemming from my experience with the crime, this one fiction.

My private determination about what would be my writerly subject certainly didn't include "true crime," or crime novels or stories at all. I was interested in character, and in a rural, agricultural, Canadian-West setting, in particular, the ranching culture I had married into; eventually, in the women of that culture. Why I stepped out of my chosen literary world to write about Alex Wiwcharuk's story is something I'm not entirely sure about. I thought about her; I couldn't stop thinking about her; one day, visiting in Saskatoon, I asked my first question.

But even then, I doubt that I would have chosen this killing as a subject for a book if I hadn't been able to still recall Alex's face clearly. We had gone to the same high school and had been in drama club and choir together for a couple of those four years. She wasn't a friend; I said hi to her when I saw her, and she to me, and that was it. She hadn't come into her adult beauty yet, didn't stand out in any way (nor did I), we were never in the same class, and I hardly noticed her except at our school Drama Night, when outside adjudicators were polite about my performances, while awarding her Best Actress two years in a row.

It was something like twenty-three years ago, when at a women's lunch in Saskatoon, and not having lived in Saskatoon for many years, I inquired in a lackadaisical way if anybody knew if her killer had ever been caught. I was told of a retired police officer who couldn't let the case go, who still wanted to know who had killed Alex. From there, I began to ask questions, getting more and more deeply involved in what was known about that night, reading the paucity of newspaper accounts of the time, reviewing whatever official documents I could get access to, interviewing people, talking with her family members and hearing their stories about Alex and about the days and weeks leading up to the night she was killed and the ensuing almost three weeks to May 30, 1962, when her body was at last found.

I can see pretty clearly now that I tackled the research with such zeal because it was, in large part, a study of my own past in Saskatoon, where we had moved in 1953, and where in 1973 my father died, and in 1987 my mother, and then one of my sisters and a niece, all buried in the same cemetery where Alex's remains lie. (To this day, when I visit my family's graves, I also visit Alex's.) Those years from 1953 to when I married for the first time in 1961 were my formative years, the ones of my youth that I remember most clearly, and not without fondness, some of them, because I was a country child seeing a city for the first time, with surprise and even awe. Later, I had much curiosity about what had become of the people with whom I went through Grade 8 and high school. By the time I began my research, not surprisingly, the city had changed greatly, the population having doubled and then some, but I found the old city, the one I grew up in, was still there, if you knew where to look. And that the locations Alex had trod through to her death that night so long ago were also still there, still the way they had been then. The research would be, for me, also a going home.

Ten years after that women's lunch, forty-six years after Alex's murder, I finally published my book *The Girl in Saskatoon: A Meditation on Friendship, Memory, and Murder,* part journalism, part memoir, and in a large part, I see now, a sort of sociology of the nineteen-fifties and early sixties for women in Saskatoon, Saskatchewan. The fact that in the couple of weeks immediately after its publication, my book sold four hundred copies in the one major bookstore in Saskatoon is proof of the community's unflagging interest in the case.

I write this essay because I'm eighty now, and because I was fourteen when I first met Alex, and because her story flared up again, unforgettable ever since she was killed at barely twenty-three, when I was twenty-two. In my 2008 book, unable to identify her killer(s), I tried instead to understand the city's enduring obsession with this crime. Now, I would like to get to the bottom of my own continuing preoccupation with it.

People still occasionally say to me, "But you barely knew her!" True, but we were members of a cohort, in a large high school attended mostly by the children of immigrants and the working-class people of Saskatoon. We were the first generation to get an education, to move up to the middle class; instead of the painters, butchers, mechanics, plumbers, construction and railway workers, and housekeepers, clerks, and waitresses our parents had been, we became successful businesspeople, university professors, artists, career professionals, and elected officials.

In those high school days, many of us had dreams of the sort our parents were in awe of or discounted as impossible. We more ambitious young women all knew that we would have to begin as teachers, nurses, secretaries, and work our way up, because our parents had no money to spare for higher education, and nothing would be given to us. Success, that is, pulling ourselves up into the middle class, depended entirely on our willingness to work very hard and our dogged determination. I was able to go to university because student loans were introduced the year I graduated from high school, and I borrowed the (then) appalling sum of $150 to add to the miniscule amount I earned working at two jobs all summer, a sufficient sum because I didn't have to pay room and board, but was allowed to live at home. I became a teacher; Alex became a nurse, which in those days didn't require more than a few dollars to start, and you lived free in a residence to graduation.

Both of us, I believe, secretly nourished much wider ambitions. I wanted to be an artist, in particular, a painter; Alex had said two years running in our yearbooks that she wanted to be a stewardess, a new, exciting profession for girls, but that demanded that you be slim and pretty (clearly, women weren't running commercial aviation companies), and also, in the first years, that you first train as a nurse. I think that she really wanted to become an actress, maybe even in Hollywood — she had proven she could act, and she was beautiful, and wonderfully vivacious, and full of charm.

I began my research into her case with the plan that I repeated endlessly to everybody, that I was only trying to find out the true story of what had happened the night she was killed, not to identify who committed the crime. I would say: "I live five hours out of the city and have no connections to help me and no training as an investigator; how can I possibly expect to find her killer(s)?" At the start, in my own mind, and for years after, even after my book was published, I reiterated this disclaimer to anybody who said I was trying to solve the case.

It was only in these last few years, as I've grown older and then older again, that I've realized that there wasn't any difference between the two aims, or what little difference there might have been existed only in my mind, because, while I might have been shockingly ambitious as a writer, I otherwise saw myself as having no agency in the world, and was also dubious about my own gifts in any direction you'd care to name. And I was also, generally, timid of authority, and specifically of the authority of the police. So, I couldn't say: "I'm here to find the killer(s)!" I would have died of embarrassment at such audacity (and I knew such an admission would be a direct challenge to the decidedly scary, all-male police force), as I was only a somewhat shy, small (an inch shorter than Alex), non-beautiful, aging white female who knew she was way out of her depth, and was, at first, anyway, scared to death about what she was trying to do.

Or did I know there was in practical terms no difference? The tortuously complicated and mostly unknowable nature of the human psyche is simply baffling: what did I know? What did I think? What was I in denial about where my real thoughts were concerned? Did I really think I could go unnoticed if I acted humbly enough and made no brazen claims? Did I really think I could map out the timeline and the actions of the principals and then stop dead at the edge of the abyss and go smugly away without naming her killer? I claimed the smaller ambition, I'm sure, because it was achievable, and wouldn't make me look like a fool trying to attain it, or so I must have thought. It was harder to fail at. Probably that was it: failure is easier to live with if you had made no grandiose claims.

And yet, remembering all those years I drove back and forth between our ranch and hay farm and Saskatoon, interviewing people and asking endless questions, and trying over and over again to see official documents and to get the police to tell me what they knew, I can actually see now that I was respected. Or, at least, was treated with some caution. Because when I think of it, at that lunch in 1998, I was fifty-eight years old, not the twenty I make myself sound like, and had (for the moment, anyway) a minor national profile, having already published a dozen books, that year won the Marian Engel Award for Women Writers in Mid-Career, a national award. And at the National Magazine Awards, again, that year, I had been shortlisted in three categories and won an honourable mention (for an article about farming), and in the same competition, also a silver in the fiction category. People sit up and take notice when something like that happens, it's hardly a commonplace, not to forget that the widely attended dinner and awards ceremony was in Toronto, abode of Canada's literary powerful. Probably most significant was that three or four years earlier, my nonfiction book *The Perfection of the Morning: An Apprenticeship in Nature* had been on the national bestseller list for a year, and had propelled me from a nobody to one who was in some demand around the country to take part in festivals, do readings and panels, and teach workshops.

While I thought I was hugely audacious to even ask questions (for the reasons mentioned above), this belief was purely a result of my own internal dynamics, and I can see now that I, or at least a part of me, was bolder and capable of acting with more cunning than I pretended to myself. I was not really a humble little dairymaid from the countryside. But I also knew that I lacked courage. My cowardice was my stumbling block, but as a result of it, trying to get around the need to be bold and demanding to find the truth, I had become a bit of a logistical thinker, and tended to use calculation to hide the failing of which I was deeply ashamed and that all my young life I had taken pains to keep hidden from my friends, although the cleverest of them had divined it, and the unkindest had openly accused me of it. But, over the years since I was a high school kid, I was beginning to understand that my amorphous, even existential fear stemmed from very early childhood wounding that had resulted in what would be called now PTSD, not the failure of moral fibre that I thought it was.

So, I faced caution in dealing with me from those who would have preferred I go back home and stay there; I also faced harassment. The harassment involved a brief period of having a tapped phone (old technology, I could hear it); being followed by marked police cars (hugely deniable, I know); once on a deserted highway after I'd just finished telling a radio host in Saskatoon on air exactly where I was, having a mud-covered car come at high speed out of nowhere to hard-ride — without ever touching — my bumper for several miles before pulling out and roaring into the distance (no witnesses); driving ten hours to meet, at his invitation, a retired police officer who, when I phoned him from just down the road that I had arrived, refused to see me, and when I protested, wanting to know why, hung up on me. The forensic professional who had taken samples from Alex's exhumed remains to get the killer's DNA, once voluble with me on the subject, later actually ran when he saw me coming, both men acting as if they were afraid of me. Or afraid of something. (Did you notice everybody in this paragraph except me was male?)

No harm was done me, though; no one searched my house or my belongings (although our local telephone repairman and installer told me when I asked him, that to tap a phone using the old technology, the installer would have to get into our house); no one "tossed" my stuff, knifed open my sofa cushions, and broke my mirrors as they always do in movies and on TV. Also, nobody beat me up, or threatened violence, only anonymously said that I would be killed if I kept on asking questions, although many years before, one of Alex's aunts was attacked in her own backyard late at night by a man with a knife — never caught of course — and her arms shallowly cut. This, among other "dirty tricks" done to the family. Notably, I could have been pushed off the road by that high-speed car, but I wasn't.

But I never forgot about the American, Karen Silkwood, who refused to let a major American plutonium company get away with union violations, and at only twenty-eight, in 1974, was killed in a "mysterious" car accident on a deserted road. So, I was upsetting people, but not enough to provoke real violence or murder. Although more amusing than sinister, the book's only bad review was published in Saskatoon, and this was at the same time as it was shortlisted for the Crime Writers of Canada's Arthur Ellis Award. To a writer, a bad review is a damaging thing, not just to the ego, but also to book sales. And yet, laughably timid compared to a high-speed multi-rollover down a country ditch.

Most people would interpret this kind of harassment as the killers secretly trying to stop investigations that might result in their being caught, while to others it looks like somebody else (read: the police) is trying to stop investigations into the case for what are surely nefarious reasons. Another interpretation though, may well be the best one: It is that the official investigators do not like amateurs messing in what they claim as their business and theirs alone. The police will tell you that homicide cases never close until the killer(s) is/are captured, tried, and sentenced. Alex's case file was and is, therefore, still closed to all but the police.

I've already written that I wasn't the most perfectly composed, mature, and brave person around, and that I wouldn't admit, especially to myself, that I hoped that my investigations would lead me to the killer. Maybe more surprising is that I wouldn't admit that I might be in real danger, if not from the still-living killer, as was suggested to me a couple of times, then from the kind of man who rode my bumper for miles on that deserted road, or the one who drove down our lane one afternoon, slowly, claiming to be lost. (In the thirty-three years I lived there, he was the only person who ever came down that trail claiming to be lost. He was clearly not a country man, and the way he examined my face with his eyes was not casual, but intense and kind of creepy.) I cannot even now think why I was so in denial about being in danger.

And yet, the day did come when I finally became afraid enough to call a national investigative television program, The Fifth Estate, which did a program and a half about the case, failing, also (which gave me — eventually — a grim satisfaction that I wasn't as dumb as they must have thought I was), to identify the killer.

Did I mention that I was told another woman had come along a year or two before I did and began to ask questions with a view to writing a book about the case, but soon gave up and went away? The retired police officer who told me this wouldn't or couldn't tell me why she quit, only shrugged and mumbled a bit when I asked. I don't know who she was, and wonder if there is a bigger story there, but have made no attempt to pursue it, and when my book was finally published, although I heard from many people who had something to say about the case, including those who had a story about that night, the writer never got in touch with me.

Interestingly, it seems that no male ever came to write Alex's story, only — as far as I know — another woman and me. I suspect that if a man had my credentials, he would have had better luck than I did getting information, although maybe not. A young reporter told me he had been threatened in the police station by an officer, although obliquely, who pointed out when he reported something they didn't like about a petty crime, that besides him, there were four hundred men in the building who would pay close attention to what he wrote. But it seems no male writer was interested enough to pursue Alex's case, and (some will be saying of me "raging feminist") even that seems to me evidence of the throwaway attitude, at least then, toward pretty young women, even one who was white, although born into a group that at that time was low on the province's pecking order, and whose family had no agency at all when it came to dealing with power.

In fact, as far as I was able to ascertain, there was not one woman involved in the work of gathering information or presenting and solving the case. All the police officers were men. The presiding official, the lawyer asking questions, and the six jurors at the coroner's inquest were all men; only — not surprisingly — the steno who took the minutes was female. Of course, Alex's three roommates, all women, were questioned, definitely not a position of power in the situation. When the *Star Phoenix* editor sent the reporter on duty to the site where Alex's body was found, the male officers there, including the police chief, would not let her do her job and sent her away, she told me this years later, because she was young and a female. As a result, the newspaper editor had to send a man to see the body and the grave and to report on the crime; the child who found her body (that is, saw Alex's hand that, so horrifyingly and pathetically, had risen out of her grave, and ran to tell others what she had seen) was a girl, not the boy the newspaper reported. (Or so she told me as an adult, still troubled from this deeply traumatizing experience.) And those who were harmed in all of this, though not involved in the case at all, were chiefly women, who then and for a long time, for years afterward, told me how they were afraid to go out at night without male escorts, and for the first time in their lives began to lock their doors, or the two who were peripheral to the killing and investigation who seem to have had breakdowns or near-breakdowns because of what they saw or knew.

Were they threatened by someone to keep silent about what they knew? If so, by whom?

As far as I can tell, since that 1962 inquest, not one of the three roommates has spoken publicly about that night. One roommate I could not find at all, one I heard couldn't bear to speak of it, suggesting, again, terrible trauma, and the third had told all she knew, or rather, all she was allowed to tell, at the inquest and I didn't try to talk to her, either. Unbeknownst to the public, legal-judicial-police jurisdictional tug of wars would have been going on behind the scene at the inquest. Fascinating for me to hear about it in a general way from lawyers and judges, but also endlessly infuriating.

In the end (suggesting, I guess, that I don't think her killer will ever be identified now that nearly sixty years have passed and most people from that time are at the least in their eighties, or else, are dead), I am surprised, when the deepest meaning of all this comes to the fore in my brain, by how enraged I am, for at least a few seconds. So furiously angered that I have to leap up from the sofa where I'm sitting and pace around, swinging my arms, my hands in fists, breathing fast and loud through my nose — me, at eighty! — until I calm down a bit, and tell myself I've always known this. But no readers seemed to notice that only men were involved in the case, not even when I wrote this fact in my book, probably because I did not bring my understanding of the forces that caused Alex to be murdered to the depth that it has reached now, and probably because I wrote weakly about what I knew. After all, girls get raped and murdered all the time, all over the world. But the more I think about the years I spent learning about human nature, and the nature of secrets and the power they grant the one who holds them, and our justice and policing system, the more I began to see how much this story is about the patriarchy itself.

Fifties girls, repressed at every turn into womanhood, once out of their parents' houses and out in the world on their own, often broke free of the rules for a while and took foolish chances and failed to understand the danger they were in most of the time, just walking down the street, never mind meeting men and going out with them. In that regard, probably beautiful girls were in greater danger. Young men knew what they had to be afraid of; young girls were often not exactly sure. I remember as a young teenager asking my mother what the word "rape" meant. I remember she looked away, her expression suddenly serious, and gave a short reply that I can't remember and that didn't explain the word; but seeing her manner, I had sense enough not to pursue the topic, and went away, a bit less mystified than I'd been when I asked her: I knew it was major, and that we didn't talk about whatever it was.

Once, in a writing workshop, a woman ten years younger than me objected to a line in a story that asserted a character, a thirteen-year-old girl, knew nothing about sex. "I guarantee she knew!" she said, and I took a shocked breath at such absurdity, squeaking out in indignation, "*I* didn't know!" Another woman, older than me, said, "I certainly didn't know," and a third agreed. That's the difference between having been a teenage girl in the fifties and one in the sixties.

Some of the story about raped and murdered girls and women is about male rage against women, but some parts of it have to do with the "good" side of the patriarchy: that because of their greater size and strength, men have understood themselves as inherently responsible for protecting women. Most of us were, and I think still are, not just accepting of this, but very grateful for it. It is only when the protectiveness eases into bullying, violence, into lying to us to protect us from eternal truths, and removing our power in the name of protection, that is, turning us into second-class citizens, that I start to get angry. More and more so the older I get. But more relevant to the investigation of Alex's death is my certainty that with a female police officer (especially one with rank), or as many of them as male officers, or a female judge at the coroner's inquest, or a female prosecutor, or a jury of women, this might all have turned out differently. Something, that, of course, I can never prove.

But women are, generally speaking in our culture, considered to focus more on compassion than men do, and to choose less often than men to screen out empathy, although there are plenty of individual cases in which this isn't true, in which even the opposite might be true. Women taking part in the inquest, perhaps also victims of male violence, of misogyny, perhaps having been sexually abused, too, even raped, would have felt viscerally what Alex had suffered, the horror of what had been done to her, that was aimed at letting her know she was nothing, that was aimed at annihilating her. I imagine that they would not have allowed the son of even the most powerful man in the country to get away with such a crime as the one against Alex, and would never have stopped trying to find who did this to her. I write this, even as I recall the decent retired male police officers I met, who did persist in pursuing Alex's case as long as they could, and I am mindful of all the decent men I've known in my life, of the fathers of daughters, of those devoted to the welfare of the women in their lives. It was the culture of the time, that women had no power outside the home. One of the tasks of the elderly is to try to sum up our lives, to make sense of them as best we can. Such an enduring theme as the murder of Alex Wiwcharuk surely matters in my life story: the ten years I spent directly researching it and writing about it, the way I still think about it so often. I need to put it in its correct place. But I don't know what that "correct place" is. I suppose I can at least say that it is the only time in my life I inserted myself into somebody else's story, somebody not a character I invented, not a family member, not even a good friend. Also, I think I was faithful in what I told about my findings to those who still cared. I have no pangs of conscience there.

Over those twenty-three years since 1998, when I began thinking about Alex's murder, I learned a lot. I learned about the corruption that seems ineradicable and exists at all levels of society, I learned about class in a society that thought itself classless, I learned about misogyny, which I had always known about, and known by name since the Second Wave of Feminism in the seventies, I learned about evil, and that it just might be incarnate. I might have grown up because of it. I might have quit kidding myself about who I am. Also, slowly, over the years, I have begun to see better what I specifically need to fear, and to separate most of that from what doesn't need to be feared. Now, at eighty, my fears come mostly (but not all) from being an old woman in an old-woman-hostile world.

Eventually, I even came to a moment when I thought (maybe even think) that I knew who killed Alex, although he is dead, and I have not a shred of proof, and without any, will never say his name. I believe, and it seems worth saying, that never, not for one second, did he forget what he did, even after the sound of her screams had faded out of his brain, long after he had washed off her blood, and the scratches and the place where she had pulled out his hair had healed. I think he didn't sleep after that, that what sleep he got was filled with her death, the feel of her face against his fist, the sound her skull made when he broke it.

VANISHED WITHOUT A TRACE

PART ONE:
WHERE I AM NOW

I had the oddest experience the other evening at a literary reading in a downtown bookstore, when a novelist began to tell me how she planned to search for a publisher for her latest novel. I couldn't immediately extract an answer out of the things I was thinking, tumultuously, several ideas wanting expression at once, and after the pause, while she waited for my answer and none came, wearing a puzzled expression, she backed away. I hadn't had even the usual two ounces of wine in the flimsy plastic glass, nor had I recently been bonked on the head, and I wasn't sleepless, nor under the influence of drugs, prescription or otherwise.

She was maybe a dozen years younger than I am, yet ours was a conversation I would have eagerly engaged in when I published my first book in 1984, when I was forty-four. Even twenty years ago, I would have said, Yes, that's how you get published! Good for you; go for it, and added the names of other publishers to her list. But I couldn't allow myself to give that straightforward, mundane answer, because I thought it wasn't true anymore; my reaction was, *my God, doesn't she know? Doesn't she realize?* referring to the fact that the publishing world has changed so drastically it's unrecognizable, that getting published is a brand-new universe, one I no longer know how to navigate. But at the same time, I realized that the old routes had, so far, worked for her (although she had never been published by a major publisher). In my own career, having been with a major publisher since the early nineties, it was branded in me that to be with a big publisher was the only goal. Further, that during the trauma of their fairly recent collapses, amalgamations, and retreat to American head offices, and their new, more stringent requirements of writers for publication (the decisive criterion now being assured high sales, it would seem, no more gambling on talent), in my scramble to keep my position with one of them, I had forgotten the old routes to publication still existed, and further, that it would be possible to go back to where I had started forty years earlier. Although, of course, I did not want to; I did not want (laughably) my failure to be public.

For forty years, I, along with nearly all of the thousands of writers out there, have been a crucial if mostly underappreciated part of the publishing pyramid, the apex of which consists of owners, below them their bureaucracy: managers, accountants, marketers and publicists, designers, layout people, and editorial staff; with writers forming the broad base on which the entire pyramid rests, and without whom the pyramid crumbles and vanishes. It's hard to believe now, but not long after I started out as the rawest beginner in 1978, I felt, if anything (and constantly glancing over my shoulder to make sure I wasn't being mistaken for somebody else), over-appreciated. How eager the country was, and our various regions were, then, for new talent, new books, new writers telling our stories.

Arts agencies, most of them provincial, had sprung up then with new funding for writers. Small publishers in the "regions" were also appearing in response to the near impossibility for so-called "regional writers" to be accepted by the few established companies in central Canada. Their operations were facilitated by grants from the federal government, newly available to Canadian-owned publishers, and the new, small publishers existed to publish the work of these writers. They did what publishers historically have always done: searched out talent and presented it to the world, their prestige as houses largely depending on the quality of the books they published, rather than strictly on sales figures. To this day, the American Sylvia Beach is remembered almost entirely because she published James Joyce's Ulysses, when no other publisher would touch it. Norman Levine — remember him? — an internationally known writer of mostly short stories, once famously wrote a story called "We All Begin in a Little Magazine," and it's true that writers still begin there — we are all grateful for the very robust magazine and journal sector in Canada — and mostly move next to the small publishers, while dreaming of the day we will be noticed by the big ones, and take the next step up the career ladder. (I remember how very angry my first publisher, owner of a tiny new company, was when I told her I now had an agent. She knew that meant I'd be leaving her soon. "I discovered you," she yelled at me. "You're mine!" The latter an argument not guaranteed to make me stay with her.) Of course, small publishers want to hang onto their most talented writers because they sell books, but also for the prestige they bring to their companies. I suppose small publishers dream of becoming big publishers, or some of them do, anyway, and of becoming powers in the publishing and literary worlds, the two not being synonymous by any means.

It has always been the case that if the rewards for an infinitesimally small percentage of writers are enormous: a clever Atwood, a genius Munro, a brilliant Ondaatje, for nearly all of the rest of us they are paltry and have little to do with the years of hard work we've done or the size of our inextinguishable desire whether for international sales, the most prestigious and lucrative prizes, or to do work held in the highest esteem by critics and (God help us, in the age of the "expert") by university professors. Even though every would-be writer has been told over and over again how poor her chances are of reaching the highest level — that of an Edna O'Brien, a Salman Rushdie, a J.M. Coetzee, a Munro or Atwood — most refuse to believe this fact applies to them. If we writers truly believed it did, we would long ago have stopped writing and retrained as lawyers, bankers, teachers, hairdressers, or nurses.

But most of us shove that grim wisdom aside to keep writing anyway, because, as some of us say, "I have to," referring to something with which I am all too familiar: an urgent need to make sense of the world on our own terms and to do it through language. In order to keep doing so, we willingly live the proverbial crusts-of-bread-in-freezing-garrets scenario, get teaching jobs to supplement our incomes, or let somebody else earn the living. I hate to say it, but I belonged to the last group, although I also worked on my husband's cattle ranch, occasionally to the point of total exhaustion, being small and non-athletic, and staying in the saddle all day for three or four days was all I could manage. As for housework, I recall one day when we had a work crew in, and I, without help, made five complete dinners, each for three to five men, including serving, cleaning, and washing up. (This after the usual breakfast for two of us, and a noon meal for four or six.) I was so tired that I actually cried. When I think of my husband's kindness to me when he saw my tears, I know he was seeing his own mother on the ranch when he was a boy.

The reason I couldn't frame a response to the novelist that night wasn't just that I had lived through the shaking up and near collapse of the big Canadian or pseudo-Canadian publishing houses, and thus had seen my own status take a nosedive, but also that I had gotten old, and the entire world was changing so fast I couldn't keep my balance anymore. Only a couple of weeks before she spoke to me, I had done a reading with the first fully transitioned man-to-woman I had ever met (as far as I know). How could someone from my era, and not raised in New York or any other big city, not have to swat down wonder?

Of course, I knew that nowadays a few people are changing their biological sex — I acknowledge that probably there have always been such people around, but I simply didn't know it — and had been astonished by this, but also accepting, if in a distant, uninvolved way. Mother Nature made lots of crazy mistakes, surely sometimes this happened, and I had tried to behave with the trans woman as if transitioning was, in my world, not only perfectly normal, but commonplace. The truth was, though, that I was jarred to my boot soles and deeply touched by her. All I could think of was how much more there is to being a woman than looking like one, even than having a vagina (as some but not all man-to-woman trans people do). What I saw was the endless pain of the endless, and universally shared, human struggle for identity. And I felt so disoriented, seeing no seamless, rational slide from the world I was born into at the beginning of World War II to this one, but instead a massive bone-crunching leap that, while willing to try, I couldn't quite make. How pleasant, intelligent, and gentle she was, how admirable in her talent and her courage.

But when the novelist leaned in and spoke confidentially to me about her plans to find a publisher, I was also still shaken by a book I had just finished: Franklin Foer's *World Without Mind*, about Facebook thieving our very lives and selling the data for incomprehensibly vast wealth, while boldly and untruthfully claiming its aims as "transparency" and "connectedness"; Google trying to steal all writers' work as if by this theft they were, out of pure magnanimity, doing the world a good deed, and Amazon, among other moves to take over the bookselling industry, discounting books so heavily as to destroy writers' incomes. I was still trying to get used to the villainy of these practices, never mind the new acceptability of self-publishing (once dismissed as "vanity" publishing), and the growing e-publishing world, not to mention the collusion of libraries — libraries! — in destroying hundreds of thousands of books to be replaced by various digitized versions, or not at all.

In trying to absorb the newness all around me, I'd been reading about: cryptocurrency (it seemed a mind-boggling delusion to me that it could be worth anything at all), the American president and the workings of his appalling mind, and what looked to be the beginning of the fall of the American hegemony in the world. I, an elderly woman, had begun to feel that I couldn't cope with this new world to which I refused to add the word "brave." I thought that the children had taken over the orphanage, that I was living in a *Lord of the Flies* universe, and I was aghast, dumbfounded, frightened, clinging as hard as I could to what I had always believed about the world, to what everybody I knew had always believed. The "me too" movement surprised me, because when I was a girl, we just knew this is how it was for females; we took the audacious moving hand, the brush up against us, or the outright attack as just what happened to everybody, and tried to keep our distance from dodgy-looking guys, and didn't tell anybody when we made a mistake, or were overpowered and raped. And worst of all, we blamed ourselves for all of that, were taught to blame ourselves! And now we could complain? We could erase our shame, and put the blame on the perpetrators? It seemed unbelievable and another thing to marvel over in this new world.

I was born in the bush country of Saskatchewan, taken from the hospital to my first home, a log house a couple of miles north of the hamlet named Garrick, after the eighteenth-century actor, theatre impresario, and playwright David Garrick, according to records of the Canadian Pacific Railroad. Then, there were virtually no roads, no electricity, no running water, let alone ensuites, and communication among nearby settlers could only occur in person.

I remember that great day when, further south in Melfort, in 1949 or '50, we got our first in-home telephone. We mischievous kids would phone random numbers and ask the person who answered certain questions, the only one of which I still remember being, "Have you got Macdonald in a can?" (meaning the ubiquitous brand of tobacco used for roll-your-own cigarettes). And when the person said yes, we kids would say, "Well, let him out, he can't breathe." Then we would hang up and would stagger around with laughter into each other and the furniture. But I was the unfortunate child who answered the phone when the operator called to tell us that she knew we were the guilty ones, and if we didn't stop at once, the telephone company would remove our phone. I remember how scared I was, too. (It occurs to me now to wonder how she knew it was us. Were we being monitored somehow even then?) Nowadays, I suppose we would have been hacking into our teachers' Facebook accounts, maybe changing exam marks, or posting nude photos of girls we didn't like. Or stealing their identities. Or urging them to commit suicide. The world I was born into had vanished, and I was out of breath, scrabbling to keep up, beginning to realize I could no longer get away with my natural reaction, which was to refuse the newness that over-whelmed me.

In the previous ten years, my books and my career had diminished in stature. For all those reasons, I couldn't begin to formulate a reasonable reply to the novelist; I simply didn't know where to begin, struggling as I was with the dawning idea that, despite my forty years of experience publishing books, I felt that world had changed so drastically as to leave me behind.

PART TWO:
I BECOME A WRITER

I started out planning to be a painter, but for reasons best left unmentioned, I gave it up and at the age of thirty-eight began to write. I began most tentatively, thinking maybe I could someday write magazine articles, although I know what I always wanted to do was write a novel. I had the first little story I wrote published, for which I was paid thirty-five dollars, and I began to see that, with my university education and the mountains of books I had read, I already had a huge advantage over many of my mostly rural, fellow aspiring writers whom I met at the handful of half-day workshops I attended. My confidence had been shoved, nearly lifeless, to the bottom of my soul by my shift from a grad student and lecturer to cattle rancher's wife, when my knowledge of that world was nonexistent. Nonetheless, at forty-four, I published my first book, a novel, and it was shortlisted for a best first novel award, and then the following year I published a short story collection that was shortlisted for the Governor General's Award for Fiction. As a writer, even though I had barely begun, I was already beginning to be noticed. Years ago, the *Globe and Mail* newspaper published a list of the ten Canadian writers under forty-five to watch for, and added a note that Margaret Atwood and I were both a year older and therefore couldn't be included. I think I grew about an inch when I saw that.

In view of such surprising, almost instant success, I had decided that, Yes! I could write. So, I told myself I would keep writing, getting better and better until I was in the first rank of writers in Canada, and then of the world. I am not kidding, or exaggerating. I believed that, if I worked hard enough, I could do it. I never breathed a word to a soul of this blossoming belief, so firmly held that it didn't quite qualify as egotism, but fell more into the category of religious belief or some kind of possibly psychotic personal mythology. Of course, I had no idea then of what the kind of writing I dreamt of doing would require of me, or even of what it consisted, but thought it was about finding the right words and placing them on the page in the most felicitous fashion. I guess I thought I was smart enough and my mind full of interesting enough ideas that I didn't have to worry about that part of the discipline. No, I think now that I thought I had the necessary vision, although, of course, I was wrong about that.

At the same time, as I barely acknowledged to myself the size of my ambition, somewhere in the darkest corners of my mind I believed that having those lofty goals was okay, because accompanying them was the equally firm commandment to myself that I could not cheat, walk over anybody, accept anybody else's ideas about how to write, not change who or what I was as a writer for money, imitate any other writer (except honourably, with acknowledgement and defer-ence), or be swayed from my purpose by all the failures I expected to endure along the way. I would educate myself in the way that the great writers of the world seemed to be educated, and that (despite nine years on a university campus), I knew I was not. I was ignorant of both how to write and of the world, but I would learn, no matter what it cost me.

I lay this manifesto out now as if I had brought it carved on a stone tablet down from Mount Olympus. Instead, it came to me gradually, step by step, most of it unconsciously, and only now that I am nearing eighty do I know that I believed it all along.

For at least thirty of those forty years, I wrote two to six hours every day, weekends and holidays included. My routine was always demanding, in summer because I rose at five when my husband did, and went straight to my desk. In the after-noon I spent three or four hours reading three, five, even six books at the same time no matter what it cost me in self-induced isolation and in the constant near-despair that I didn't have what it took after all. I didn't examine the new ideas about the illegitimacy of the concept of "great-ness," "greatness" being a fixed idea my generation grew up with, and in which we'd been educated. I believed, too, that being an artist was a precious gift, the worth of which was unmatched and bled into the spiritual world. I thought artists were blessed. As utterly grandiose as all this sounds now, not to mention naïve, I admit that I mostly still believe it, but, of course, always in a better world than this one. I don't know if it is crazier, given where I came from, to have ever believed it, than to be unable fully to shake those convictions even now.

Early on in my self-education, suspecting I would be dismissed because I had come out of poverty and the furthest boonies, I sought to find out about the lives of the great writers back into the nineteenth century. I was not happy to discover that most of them lived in cities, mostly came from the upper middle class or higher, and had the fanciest of educations, as well as being, almost all of them, males. These facts brought home to me that I was a cliché, the poor kid from the backwoods who thought she could make herself as worthy a writer as a countess or one of the New York City Four Hundred families or central Canada's private school crowd who ran our country, and who took it for granted from birth that they would. I would outdo all of them with my talent and my unflagging, hardest work.

Trying to be canny about my career, I also decided that I would not write willy-nilly as the inspiration hit me, but would find a world and become its chronicler. The world of the rural agricultural people of Western Canada was a natural choice, because I lived in the middle of it, and through my marriage had a rare, privileged view of it, and I wouldn't be treading on any other writer's turf, as no one was writing about it in a committed, continuous way. I knew that choice would make everything harder, because most readers are urban and have less interest in the lives or work of Canada's rural inhabitants. I vowed that I would change that by writing so well about life in the country that urban readers would find it as fascinating, heartbreaking, noble, and beautiful as I did, as much so as the world of royal courts and great cities and universities. I had come out of a working-class family, my father a sometime lumberjack and short-lived mill owner with a grade-school education, while my mother had been taken out of high school by her parents (unnecessarily according to her sister), and all her life yearned for and revered education. I knew first-hand what the men, women, and children of that world went through: they would always come first in my loyalties.

Thus, I wanted to be a female Thomas Hardy (*Tess of the D'Urbervilles*) or a female Knut Hamsun (*Wayfarers*) or a female Patrick White (*The Tree of Man*), but to write about the women, as Olive Schreiner did (*The Story of an African Farm*), not about the men. I paid my dues to the men in my early novel *The Gates of the Sun*, for which I had spent hours listening to the stories of an old cowboy as well as many from my husband and his friends, and used some of the most scandalous ones. Better yet, I wanted, I have always wanted, to write my own *Madame Bovary*, for did I not live among such women? Was I not one myself? I think Olive Schreiner might have been one, too. All of us lost on African farms, Canadian ranches, the suburbs of North America, yearning for more exciting and more glamorous, more meaningful lives.

I continued to refuse every hint that I was destined for disappointment and failure, but I was often, despite myself, worried about the bargain I thought I had struck. I read Nicholas Boyle's two-volume biography of Goethe and studied Goethe's play *Faust* and Thomas Mann's version, *Doctor Faustus*, and Christopher Marlowe's seventeenth-century *The Tragical History of Doctor Faustus*. Faust wanted riches, the most beautiful women, and all the knowledge of the world. I was not so ambitious: I wanted only to be a great writer. I noted over and over again that I was a woman, and they were men; Faust was a man. I never saw clearly that I was living in the midst of a profound cultural shift, which was a powerful cry for inclusivity set against the devaluing of the notions and efforts of the "great" white males, but I continued to think that the culture I had been raised in and lived in was still best and would triumph.

Once, while taping a television interview, I was asked, "What did you give up for writing?" Stricken to the core by the unexpected question, I replied not emphatically, but softly, looking away, "I gave up *everything* for writing." The room was silent, the interviewer motionless. He did not say, "What is 'everything?'" as if he knew, or perhaps he could not conceive of someone giving up everything. Or perhaps he was confused by my claim. My answer had been so spontaneous that I wasn't sure I knew myself — if he had asked me — how to answer him. Everything: family, life, fun — *freedom* — I cannot bring myself to answer that here. Facing this question directly in those seconds, I don't think it even occurred to me that I might have been wrong — or, it occurred to me, but I suppressed the thought at once.

The day I received a phone call telling me that my first collection of short stories, *Queen of the Headaches*, was short-listed for the Governor General's Award, instead of being elated, I fell instantly into a deep depression, as if the weight of the nomination was too heavy to bear, but what I was thinking was, *No, no, it is too soon, I haven't earned it yet.* I thought if such a nomination was that easy to attain, it was not what I thought it was at all; it meant that the whole foundation of my desire was only air, dependent on the whims of others and on some kind of weird luck. Even at the very beginning, I knew that I did not want to reach the top by luck, nor with superficial, trendy, or high-rhetoric, but trivial, work. I should have known then what would follow in the years to come, but I was lost in my generation's ideas of greatness and what a lifetime of work and purity of desire might achieve. I wonder now if, given my tendency to know some things before they happen, what so depressed me was simply that I knew at once that I wouldn't win. Margaret Atwood won for *The Handmaid's Tale*.

I wonder now, if I knew then that I would never win, that the bargain I thought I had made was either a pathetic joke, or that it was far bigger, deeper, and more serious than I could ever have imagined. In that moment my soul knew what it would cost, and even that failure was assured, and that all of this striving would one day crush me. I could carry on, but only by denial. But I recall one night, deep in thought about my vastly audacious promises to myself that my moral stance was questionable: I had a husband, a child who needed me, a commitment to work in the ranching enterprise, as well as a mother and sisters and even friends, to all of whom I owed loyalty and the willingness to help when needed. I said to myself that should any one of them need me, I would give up writing for them, smugly assuring myself that I was, after all, a decent woman, a fine woman, and not one of those monsters of desire.

I was alone in my office in the luminous shadows just before night fell, and an axe came down from above, and split me open from the top of my skull to my pubic bone. With this bloodless, painless vision came the absolute knowledge that I was a liar. That I would always put my writing ahead of any other significant demand on me; that there was nothing and nobody for whom I would stop.

My head fell forward, my face pushed against the Formica-covered surface of the homemade table I used as my desk. I remember that, overshadowing my amazement at the manner of the revelation, was growing horror that I was after all a bad person, and more: that I had put myself in such a situation — being judged by what seemed to be a disembodied moral authority outside myself — realizing that I had not known the seriousness of what this unquenchable, ferocious desire of mine, this pact I had made, had gotten me into. I was appalled, frightened, and, indeed, scared to death. I'd been raised a Roman Catholic, so, on one hand was destiny, and on the other, damnation. To truly understand this revelation would have required that I know things about myself that I wouldn't know until now, when I am at the near-end of my life. I am sure that I thought my desire wedded to my pledge to become worthy of its fulfillment was noble and put me in a higher class of humanity than the people with whom I spent my days: the cowboys, farmers, and ranchers who ignored me or kept a good distance; the hard-working decent farm wives who mostly despised me so I kept away from them; the drifters, people who, though not born there, not knowing rural or small town life, though with PhDs or money or their own brands of craziness, often wound up living as solitary ghosts in the remote villages of our vast, empty district.

Now that I know that within the terms I had set for myself, I have failed, I ask myself, did I really want that Olympian aim of greatness? Yes, I used to say to myself. No explanation required. But, surely, also, I suspect my desire has a bigger meaning, and goes back into what Jung called "the collective unconscious," into mythology, and perhaps even the world of dreams and visions. Maybe all of us want our own versions of what I wanted, but, facing the enormous obstacles and hardships that such a desire requires for success, most of us instead are satisfied with ordinary, unremarkable lives. I suspect that nearly everybody feels this way, and that I am the oddity, the crazed person. Or, thinking of the many writers I have known, perhaps not.

But now, forty years later, of course I know that the more mundane answer to the question of where my ambition comes from goes back to my childhood and must have had to do with emerging from it feeling I was nothing, had no rights and no value: being part of a tiny fringe of Catholics in Protestant towns, being half French where British people who mostly despised the French held sway in all the ways that mattered, being the second child of five. (Surely, I had bolstered this feeling by making choices in adulthood guaranteed to fulfill this teaching.) I did not even know how very angry I was, and when I saw that rage in other writers I knew, I was frightened by it and even silently condemned it in them. What fakes we writers are!

I think from early childhood, the idea that I was *not* nothing must have stirred inside me, incoherent and far below my consciousness. As I grew into adulthood, my handicaps were great: I was a young female in the repressive white-glove-wearing 1950s, I was only five feet tall, I was not beautiful, and mostly due to poverty, I had never had any opportunity to exercise and develop whatever gifts I had. And the fragility of my psyche was something I would become conscious of much, much later.

All those factors were not necessarily enough to cause serious psychological trauma — the world is full of women like me: too small or too big, ordinary to look at, smart and talented, but without agency in the world. The specific trauma came from something I never told my parents, although I believe my father discovered it and kept it from my mother (because it must have happened on his watch), which in turn caused her to dislike me for my odd, unpleasant behaviour as a toddler, the cause of which she did not know; and having by then three children, one of them disabled, another on the way, and a fifth in the future, she turned away from me. And being so young when it happened — I believe a sexual attack of some kind and degree — I did not know it myself until both my parents were long dead, my much-loved father even calling back from the grave to try to tell me. But only after several years of thought and inquiry did I understand his most cryptic message, I think this dark secret provides an explanation as to why I chose the most elevated belief, especially when I came from nowhere and had nothing much to recommend me, no reason to think myself capable of anything out of the ordinary, other than my designation at school as one of the smart kids.

But the night the axe split me down to my fundament, shocking me as hard as if the blow had been actually physical, and causing me consternation, anguish, a wavering, awed disbelief and more, I could not then resolve the wisdom given me. I had to have thought that I could not solve the problem of my cruelty and weakness inherent in this bold aim of mine, the inevitable accompaniment to the other side of my enormous desire, by simply giving up writing. I could not fully imagine that as a possibility. I had to have believed that being the very best writer was far more valuable than being a quiet, dutiful housewife and helper of others. Somewhere in all of this mess, I had to have believed that.

No wonder visions occasionally came to me; I had a mind that allowed them, and even needed them, knowing also that trauma can do that to you, too. Now I see, as well, what I had never thought of: I loved writing; I loved it as much as my husband loved his cattle and his horses and his grass, which he had so easily attained as his birthright — not that his lot was easy, it wasn't; it was very hard, if differently from the difficulty of what I chose. But he was them; they were him. I wanted the same for myself; I wanted to *be* my writing, although no one would ever give that to me, that identity I had to build for myself. And I had to have believed that I would never be challenged to choose between writing and the needs of anyone I loved or had responsibility for. Or, more likely, that I would get by without being challenged. In fact, in the years that followed, I was challenged three times: one I refused completely; one I halfway met, and one I gave myself fully over to. Is that a fail or a pass? I had been given three chances to prove my worth, and I finally met one of them. Nonetheless, the metaphoric axe had revealed a truth, and I knew I should do — something — I couldn't even bring myself to say what it was I should do. I settled for not thinking about it.

I reached the peak of my success when I was in my sixties: another Governor General's Award shortlist nomination, for nonfiction, came in 1994, and was won by a man I'd never heard of, and who, as far as I know, was never heard of again in the literary world. I also became a finalist for a regional Commonwealth Writers' Prize for fiction. Alice Munro won that one. In my seventies, I once again became a finalist for the Governor General's Award for nonfiction, which a man won, again, someone I hadn't heard of, although I was told he is an American (maybe he is a dual citizen). My 1994 nonfiction book, which spent a year on the Canadian bestseller list, won Saskatchewan's nonfiction prize, but alas, not the award for Saskatchewan's Book of the Year. That book did win in another category, one that had to be invented — "Spirit of Saskatchewan" — of which mine was the only entry, and which, as far as I know, was never offered again.

For me, though, the highest moment came one day when I wandered into a chain bookstore on Queen Street in downtown Toronto and saw along the back wall from floor to ceiling, in a stand I recall as being maybe six feet wide, many copies of my then-current book, front covers out, side by side. But not long after that, a major distributor collapsed, and as a result my book vanished from the shops. And yet, the sales in Canada were impressive, a significant number: my dreams were coming true — weren't they? Instead of things growing more wonderful, though, new factors were creeping into the literary scene and were beginning to affect my career.

PART THREE:
THINGS START TO GO SIDEWAYS

At the same time as my upward momentum was slowing, many new young writers were coming on the scene, including many talented writers, some of colour, from different cultures, newcomers to Canada or not, and were being accepted at last, so that the competition for publishers and the reading public was getting stiffer and stiffer. My sales record was still good

VANISHED WITHOUT A TRACE

enough to get me a publisher, but my ten percent wouldn't pay the rent, and the big-money prizes continued to elude me. In the meantime, filmmaker after filmmaker took options on my material, all of which lapsed without anything further happening. Eventually, I had books published in four or five languages; two were taken on by the prestigious publisher Virago, in England, and one was published *twice* in the United States. After the miniscule initial payment, I don't think I received another penny from any of them. My plan had been to write each book better than the last one, building to a breathtaking brilliance, but instead, I remember saying to my then-editor that I was growing afraid I was becoming one of those writers who regularly churned out acceptable book after acceptable book, each one to mild interest and milder praise, and each soon forgotten. And with each book, those authors, as I was, were a couple of years older.

I could see, also, that to most academics and prize-giving juries, I was stuck as not a winner but an also-ran, a not-quite-good-enough, as each year I got older and then older again, and I am sure the pernicious effects of ageism also began to kick in, because most of the editors at publishing houses, and editors of literary magazines in general, were at least a generation younger than me. No, I'm not looking for pity or praise or comfort, nor looking to be forgiven. I'm no longer enraged about my failure to reach pinnacle of my profession. My story is far from unique, and I suspect that parallels exist in many fields of endeavour in and outside of the arts.

There I was, in my sixties and stalled as a so-called midlist author, and destined — short of an act of God — to remain one for the rest of my career. But I couldn't accept that I wouldn't be rewarded with more success after giving everything I had to what I thought was the highest calling, like in fairy tales, mythology, and some religious belief systems, and in popular cant, after years of hard labour and frequent near-despair. I realized that great wealth, the highest accolades, and the accompanying reverential status was turning out to be a pipe dream.

In the midst of the changing literary world (of which I was barely aware), in August 2007, when I was still sixty-six, on the midlist, doing all right, and still hopeful of rising higher, personal catastrophe struck in the death of my husband. He was my second husband, but we had been married for thirty-one years and together longer. During the first year after Peter died, I couldn't read, write a word properly, or even watch television because the pictures made no sense to me. But, a nonfiction book, *The Girl in Saskatoon*, already well in process, was published just six months after Peter's death in the spring of 2008.

When he became officially ill, I had cancelled all my engagements to stay by his side; a mere two months later, he was gone. But the literary world treated me as if I was the one who had died. At first, I'm sure they were being respectful and protective, but rather than calling me to write a story for a magazine or newspaper, they called someone else. In no time, I also stopped receiving invitations to literary festivals and conferences. I might even have been grateful that the pressure was off, at least for the first couple of years of the next seven.

My next book, a novel, was published in 2015. In the face of my apparent vanishing from the literary world, I knew while I was still working on it that it was quite likely, even probable, that no big publisher would touch it. I decided that therefore there was no point in writing for their editors or for the reading public they were trying to attract. Instead, I would write the novel about a woman that I had always wanted to write. But *now* she would not be a feckless, foolishly impassioned, reckless, and eventually pathetic, even tragic, Madame Bovary as I thought for so long I wanted to write, but a strong, clever woman in the mold of those I had known as Western pioneers: my mother, my aunts, my grandmothers. I felt profound liberation in that decision, but the outcome was the same: a small, if truly devoted mostly sixtyish female readership. Why is that not worth anything?

When I came back from my widow's hiatus, the publishing industry had become unrecognizable. Proof of this enormous change came in several forms, but the best evidence, reported in 2018 by the Writers' Union of Canada, had to do with remuneration for writers. Our incomes had dropped twenty-seven percent since 1998; eighty-one percent of writers now had incomes below the poverty line; worse, female writers now earned fifty-five percent of what male writers earned. But with my husband's death, I became the sole owner of a bank account that, if it did not make me rich, left me able to live as I always had, a way that had never involved lavish spending or luxuries, but that did not require getting a job as a greeter at Walmart. This was untrue of hundreds of writers who had no choice but to bend to the digital barbarians, or go back to university to learn to code, or find a job that paid a regular salary, who then wrote on weekends and holidays and, after a while, not at all.

Constant rejection for reasons I couldn't understand, thinking I was alone in this, caused me to undergo almost complete breakdown of my faith in myself as a writer. But at a book festival party on one of the Gulf Islands, a writer I thought of as a Canadian icon swivelled her head around when she overheard me say, "I have lost my confidence." "Me too!" she said. "I too have lost my confidence!" I wondered privately, full of terror, whether it was possible to lose your talent. At another conference, a writer who had once received the highest accolades told me of his latest manuscript, "It's my best work, and I can't find a publisher." I was in complete, if helpless, empathy with him.

We didn't want to believe the midlist was gone, because that meant a denial of everything we believed in, that had sustained us through all sorts of travails and heartbreak. We thought it was a denial of literature itself. We couldn't believe it, not when James Joyce had been published and eventually celebrated, and four hundred years after his death Shakespeare was still a big seller, and eighteenth-century Jane Austen's works had become twentieth-century block-buster films, and while none of these works saw international bestseller status (or its equivalent then) in their authors' lifetimes, all of them helped to form the very foundation of our culture.

Never mind that vast companies were determined to reduce intellectual property to the status of shoes and car parts. Despite their colossal wealth and power, some of us found these corporations' leaders laughable, these left-brained, isolated, nerdish kids who thought they had the answers to all the ills of the world. We thought *they were* the ills of the world.

What was it we had believed? In its loftiest terms, that literature was about truth, that it was meant to be a revelation about the way the world is, that its goals were to help the human race slowly to rise out of the primeval slime into full personhood and spiritual understanding. At our best, we wrote to enhance understanding and to alleviate suffering. All that destroyed? Gone? Vanished forever? I was beginning to have flashes of the way I was guilty of still living in that old world and that just possibly my incomprehension, born of refusal, was what was destroying me. Or maybe it was worse: Maybe it was the sorrow of elderly people in general, that having been born of another age, I could not remake myself to fit the new one.

PART FOUR: I EMERGE AGAIN

But the novelist in the bookstore had leaned toward me in a confidential way, talking about what publishers she thought she would approach with her book, as if nothing had changed since 1984, and I was stunned that somewhere out there — the small presses, the university publishers — a world still existed like the one that existed when I had begun to become a writer. I couldn't figure out what to make of that; I didn't know whether to be heartened or disheartened by it. I wondered where literature would reside now.

But, I told myself, good books still do get published to an international audience, and do win the most prestigious prizes. Most often, it seemed to me, the people who won them were around the age I was when, over forty years earlier, in my thirties, I had started writing. At last I was forced to face the question: Was it really that I was simply *not good enough?*

For the first many years, I knew that I wasn't, but accompanying this thought was always "yet," and the vow to work even harder. I would remind myself of all the writers I knew who had started out with me but had stopped writing. Experience was teaching me that most of the hottest new writers only lasted *at that peak* a few years — "my fifteen minutes of fame" a new major-prize-winner said to me — before sliding back into the regular, plodding career of most of us, although their names would still hold enough *cachet* to keep their books at a big publisher. I read the books of the literary world's latest discovery, and knew that I could never have come up with whatever that writer was doing that was original, that proverbial "fresh voice." But fresh voices had nothing to do with what I had been aiming for; they belonged to some other category of writing, or so I told myself. I was reminded that Margaret Laurence, once this country's top writer, is virtually ignored today; the same is true of Robertson Davies, who was once a huge hit; I read that Patrick White, awarded the Nobel Prize for Literature in 1973 (and whom J.M. Coetzee, himself a Nobelist, describes still as Australia's greatest writer), is today largely forgotten in Australia. I kept remembering, not very willingly, that a hundred years passed after Shakespeare's death before his reputation began to grow outside of England, or possibly outside of London, and that David Garrick, eighteenth-century actor and theatre impresario, was in good part responsible for this through producing his plays. Mostly, I felt anguish (a step beyond sheer denial, though), about what had happened to my writerly dreams. I was seventy by then, and then seventy-five.

I had published three more books since the one that came out immediately after my husband's death, bringing the total to twenty with two more on the way to publication, and I am working on another. Despite being nearly at the end of my seventies, I was — I am — still in good health, and looking pretty good for my years, or so everyone tells me. My burst of late life creativity is surprising to everyone, and I laugh and say, "I haven't much time left; I have to get everything down before I depart," although what keeps me writing is the same motive that I began with: I continue to have ideas that I need to explore through writing. I can see no reason to quit, for what else would I do with myself? After years of the hardest struggle, the misery of it, the pain and the doubts each day as I tried to find the right words for the idea whose shape I was struggling to reveal, writing is coming easily now, and flows.

Then, in 2018, forty years after I began writing, I won an award designated for "emerging writers." As the saying goes, I didn't know whether to laugh or cry, although I was in fact, too astonished to do either, but in the end, decided to simply accept the honour — my only other choice being indignantly to refuse it, which would have been even more humiliating — once it was explained that "emerging" meant somebody who has never won a national or a top provincial award. Yup, I thought, that's me. It would be difficult to find a crueller way, although it wasn't meant as such, to have to face that, despite having given everything I had to writing, I was not, I would not be, one of the chosen. I lacked some spark of genius or of originality, or else I needed a higher degree of wisdom — I knew I could now write sentences and paragraphs — and there wasn't the time left to acquire it. My dream had ended.

I thought then of what my life might have been like if I had not decided to give everything over to the goal of being a writer of the highest order, if I had not bothered to try to expand and deepen my education about what it is to be human, if I had made these decisions earlier and had not tied myself first to one husband and then to another. If I had not been a mother. If I had been a man. If I had known how to keep separate my life as a person, a female, a lover, a mother, a social creature, from my creative life as a writer. If I had been born into a wealthy family. If I had been tall. If I had had the best education. If I had been born where there was opportunity, instead of where there was not. If I had been a different personality than the one I became. If I had been somebody else, in another place.

I often thought, too, of my first home, an electricity-less, running-water-less log house on the edge of the boreal forest of Saskatchewan, near the hamlet the CPR named after the incomparable David Garrick. Although others insist that the village was named after an early settler, someone about whom no one knows a single detail and who, if he ever existed, has vanished without a trace.

But, as years continued to pass, I remembered another stream of thought that seemed to me to be designed for those of us who were talented but came from the remote countryside and thus did not belong to the urban literati or to any useful cliques, were not backed by a university, and lacked a wealthy family, influential connections, the best education, or any particular luck. This line of thinking goes: if you are unsullied by working solely for material reward or for prestige, if you remain true to your goals — your bargain with yourself — and do not flag in your work in the face of failure after failure, the day will come when success will come to you. *But it will not come until you cease to care if it does or it doesn't.* And it may not come in the way you had envisioned it. This thought brought a wry smile to my face, because I knew damn well the day would *never* come when I no longer cared if I got published, or won prizes and became famous, or could live with a little luxury from my writing income. But a part of me knew at once and knows right now that this idea of success coming from relentless, pure striving, truer than the first, that of the Horatio Alger–Dick Whittington daydream that apparently motivated the British (in their class-bound society?) and Americans (and me), that persisted for at least a hundred years, until today when the American Dream of people from the lowliest beginnings being able to reach the top is largely dead. Although some of the loudmouths south of the border insist that the American Dream is alive and well, I think we have enough evidence — and success comes in part out of luck and being in the right place at the right moment.

But I also think that the idea of earning one's way, of making one's self worthy of the great rewards through purity, truth, hard work is buried deeply in the human psyche. I think it means something much more than it seems to, but I leave that discussion to theologians and philosophers, because those questions are spiritual. If the bargain is steadfastly maintained in the face of every loss and sorrow and even the encroachments and devastations of old age, if it is truly *earned*, what comes is indeed a kind of success, but not the kind dreamt of by the illusion-ridden, starry-eyed girl-woman so many years ago. And, yes, I know, that one is the more valuable.

But, drifting to sleep one night, I found myself thinking about one of my long-dead sisters, smiling to myself at how funny she could be, remembering how she suffered. I searched my memories to see if I had forgotten important things about the way she had been. But when I got to the real person, there was no one there at all; it was as if my dear sister had never existed, and I was shocked, and thought in wonder that perhaps it was true, that maybe she had never existed. That she herself was only her own dream of herself. That the wisdom I had sought since I was a child, and all those many years of seeking, all the pain, loss, and failure that came with it, came down to this, I thought, that we are all of us, in the end, only dreams of ourselves. Is that what Shakespeare meant when he wrote, "We are such stuff as dreams are made on," and I was never sure who he meant was dreaming?

I was exchanging my consuming ambition, my drive for the highest excellence, my need to be *in* and part *of* the world for the simple truths of the order of things, and for a depth of wisdom I had been unable to reach through study and through writing, and that I had hidden from myself in willful blindness. I was going the way of everyone, and one day I thought, what is this, if it isn't the story of a life, anyone's life?

DOING THE RIGHT THING

When I came in from outside and saw that I had several voice messages on my phone, I pushed the button to hear them before I'd even taken off my walking shoes. I knew at the first intonation that my young relative was calling, and by the number on the phone, although I didn't recognize it, that it was a local call. Sweat broke out on my forehead and palms, and I tensed, listening as intently as I would if the message were warning me that a missile was about to hit my building and I should run for my life. I erased the messages and hung up the phone. At once it began to ring again. I backed away from it, involuntarily hunching, hands going up to cover my ears, arms bent and pressed against my ribcage as if to protect my breasts and heart, until, finally, the ringing stopped. It rang another three times before I went to sleep, and each time without even looking at the number I knew it was the young relative again. In bed, I lay flat on my back, motionless, eyes open, staring at the ceiling until it finally stopped.

I knew she was desperate. I knew that public opinion would say that I was an unfeeling monster for not answering the phone, not driving downtown at once to pick her up from some dive or off the street wherever she was. I also knew that she would be somewhere I wouldn't have even known existed before she had summoned me to it, and that this scene would be something I would forever after have to suppress from my memory. All night I felt as if I were a prisoner in a condemned cell, that there was no escape, that she would find me, and my life would go back to being safe and regular only now and then, each time for a bit, before she found me again. That if I saw her — I could imagine the condition she would be in — I wouldn't be able to stop myself from offering whatever comfort she wanted, even though I knew she would steal small items from my house to sell for cash to buy alcohol or maybe drugs; I knew, too, that once she had found out my address, she would tell her dangerous, down-and-out acquaintances, people she had probably met not minutes earlier, from the downtown bars or on the street, and they would come and try to get into my building, and that I would be, more or less, not only endangering myself, but also my fellow residents, many of them elderly single women like me. That I had had all I could take; that I would not rescue her anymore, even though I knew her parents were dead (she was in her late thirties by now), that she had no siblings, and no one else in our family would even take her calls anymore, and kept their addresses unknown to her. They did this because she would come; she would demand; she would make their lives a horror until somehow, from somewhere, she would get a better offer and would vanish again without so much as a thank you, or notice, or a hug, but instead, with a glance of amused contempt at me or them as she walked briskly away to the dubious-looking guy revving his beater at the curb. Through the side window we would see her laughing, as he whined out, tires smoking, laying down rubber.

My selfishness astounded me; I would never have dreamt I would come to this, but I kept telling myself, fist pressed against my mouth as in the background the phone rang and rang, that she would soon give up, that she would stop phoning me, she would do what she always did when desperate, which was to find a man who would feed her and — if he had one — give her a bed to sleep in. For which, he would exact a price I couldn't bring myself to think about, but that, for her, I supposed, would just be life on the street for a female.

I had always come to her rescue when, at eighteen or twenty, she called me, sobbing because she had been thrown out of her alternative school and training program, even though she had been told that one non-compliance, she would be out; there would be no second chances; or at around sixteen or seventeen, when she showed up with cigarette burns on her face and refused to tell me who had done it, or in what situation, so that I could only nurse her, and as soon as the burns started to heal and could be hidden with thick makeup, despite my protests, she left again; or when, at twenty-two or twenty-six or twenty-eight, having been evicted from her apartment for having parties — "every single night," one landlord said — she had nowhere to go and not a penny to her name or a stick of furniture. Once, although a police officer acquaintance had told me not to go to a certain building she more or less lived in without a police escort, I went anyway, because she had called and was not in her right mind.

Now I repeated to myself: she is not a child anymore. It's her life; she is responsible for her life, not me. Everything I do only helps her for the moment, she doesn't change, whatever it is this time will only happen again in a week or a month, and to help her is a waste of my diminishing resources and energy. I have done everything I can. I washed my hands, but in my heart those hands dripped blood, even though I had stopped believing the message of Christian charity; I wasn't going to be licking the sores of any leper ever again. I had had enough. But my gut clenched, and I fought down nausea, while in the background the phone kept ringing.

The next day I spent out of my condo as much as I could, because listening to the phone ring and refusing to allow myself to answer it while assailed by unrelenting guilt was too hard. Remembering her pale skin, the tiny freckles on her nose, and as she grew into adolescence, her mane of silky dark hair, her blue-green eyes flecked with amber and fringed with thick lashes, remembering too how bright she had been before she reached puberty. Then she became delinquent, and not long after turned into a madwoman. I thought of the teachings of the nuns and priests who had been influential in my childhood, I thought of all the saints out there who would condemn me, and I put my metaphoric hands against my ears and walked as fast as I could in the other direction. Even though by refusing her, I was the criminal, not her, and I knew it.

But when I returned in the late afternoon, again there was a phone message, this time from a Mountie asking me to return his call as soon as I received it. He explained that he had picked her up on the highway on the edge of a town I hadn't heard of, but that he said was not more than a hundred miles from my home. He seemed to think, because she had told him so, that I would come to pick her up. I asked him some questions — did she have any money, was there a vial of pills in her purse — he said no to both — and after a bit of discussion about ways we might resolve the situation, he put her on the phone with me. She didn't cry or beg or wheedle. Instead, she was furious with me, berating me for not answering my phone all the times she had called, and when, cravenly, I said I had been away, she knew I was lying. She was a master liar herself, yet her disgust with me was palpable. When I said that no, I wouldn't come for her, she hung up on me. As always, I was a monster if I didn't help her, but a mere means to an end if I did.

Oddly, or maybe it wasn't odd, she felt she was owed my help, but any responsibility of hers to me simply didn't exist. Gratitude didn't seem a concept she was aware of. Even the human need to be loved mattered to her only when she was so broken (for the moment) that she was like a helpless child. I knew myself, finally, after years of her crises, during which she began abject, childlike, and emotionally resourceless (less and less so as the years passed), and under my care slowly came back to that relentless, driven, fearless self, to be completely unable to effect any difference in her lifestyle or her way of thinking about it.

When the Mountie came back on the line, I said, "I bet you think I'm a mean old woman to just send her back."

I was surprised when he answered, "No, ma'am, I think you are doing exactly the right thing." But I needed to explain. "I'm in my seventies now," I told him, "my husband is dead, I am alone, and I can't do this anymore." I didn't ask to speak to the young relative again, she wouldn't have taken the phone anyway, unless I would say I'd changed my mind and would be there in a couple of hours. I couldn't have guessed this would be the last time in our lives that I would hear her voice.

Later, seeking absolution for my cruel deed, I told a friend, who had for thirty-plus years been a social worker, what I had done. She said that our province's current political regime would have cut every benefit to even the most distressed, but didn't only because it wouldn't be reelected, so even though my relative was one of the unemployable, she wouldn't receive enough benefits to survive in even the most meagre way, and I was therefore right to have sent her back to a province where social service support was higher. As well, my friend pointed out, our city was four times the size of hers, and the petty criminals on skid row, or whatever the place where the down-and-outers live out their lives is called these days, would "eat her alive." If I was dubious about the latter, when I considered even the paltry amount I knew of crime, drug abuse, gangs, human trafficking, and the sex trade in our city, I thought my friend must be right.

In all of this, I felt tremendous relief that I had steeled myself and stayed resolute until the very moment the Mountie took her to the bus station in the town near where he had found her and made sure she picked up the ticket that I had paid for so that she could return to where she had come from.

The Mountie promised me that a colleague would come by the station and make sure she got on the bus. But in the night, I lay awake, unable to suppress my memories of the little girl I had loved, her sweetness, her quickness and intelligence, and the feel of her small hand in mine, and tossed in bed, because I felt I hadn't done enough, and wondered what people who were better than I am would have done. I also knew that the combination of human rights legislation — I could not *make* her do anything — and privacy laws meant that I knew next to nothing about her life or treatment. In the past, my husband and I, with deepest sincerity, had offered her a permanent home with us. Instead of being pleased or grateful or happy, she physically edged away from us, and in mere days went back to the city. But I knew that in her late teens she had been diagnosed as schizophrenic, and given drugs she mostly didn't take, so any notion of her having chosen her life on the streets was far from true.

About the time she ran away from us at fifteen, I had begun sometimes to notice, when she didn't know I was watching her, her eyes grow dark, harden, and become fixated on something only she could see. Some drive had, in those moments, overtaken everything she knew and had been taught to believe about life. Her drive for this one thing, whatever it was, I recognized as unstoppable. I should have known then that no matter what I did for her, how gently I talked to her and tried to teach and show her, while giving her the things she needed to lead a normal life, she would spurn it all; she would do what she would do. But I kept answering the phone year after year. Even when I knew very well who was calling me.

Over the years, I had grounds to have her committed a total of five times and for five different reasons, one of the worst being when she had endangered her dying mother's life by shutting off her oxygen generator in the night because the noise bothered her. Her mother couldn't get out of bed or walk at all anymore, and lay in bed gasping until I came in early that morning and found her. I knew at once that having my relative committed was my only solution. By the time I met her with the two police officers at the hospital intake, I was shaking too hard to put the right coins into the dispenser to get her the Coke she wanted. Someone else had to pick them out of my hand and put them in the machine. A part of me stood back and watched me, pointing out that this situation was not about me, but I couldn't stop shaking anyway. Guilt and shame can do that to you; I was never afraid of her, though I knew some others were.

Once I found out that she was on the street in a different city, with her toddler. I could not allow that to happen, and so called the police, explained the situation, and two cars pulled up to where she stood on the street, one a police car picking her up to take her to the hospital where she would spend the next five or six weeks, and the other to take her child into temporary care. Once she left the hospital, she seemed to have forgiven me for that, or maybe she had been so ill that she didn't remember what had happened. After her release, she did what she could to get back her child. The other three times, she was on the street and so delusional that when she talked to me over the phone, I knew I had to get her help at once.

After that time, I was invited in to her meeting with her psychiatrist and listened to him as he quietly, gently, without disapproval or apparent disbelief, questioned her about how she knew a particular event (delusional in nature) had happened, until, as he unravelled her current story thread by thread, I, too, could feel her delusion leaking away. We three sat in perfect silence for a few moments. I wondered why I was there and thought it must be so he could show me how to handle these incidents. I couldn't think of any other reason, although, of course, I knew I was under scrutiny, too.

My interventions usually took most of a day spent on the phone, and cost considerable amounts of money, relaying her circumstances, and then repeating them again, to various authorities: the police, her social worker, crisis-line workers, and whoever would help me get her to a safe place. Once, when she escaped from the police, or wasn't where I had told the police they could pick her up, I wound up driving five hours to her city, and going on my own to the parking lot of the biggest mall close to the bus station, where I was sure I would find her. It occurs to me now that even with her constant lies, her playacting, her occasional lawbreaking, her delusions, there was a buried level where she was uncomplicatedly still a delinquent adolescent in her behaviour. I had said to the psychiatrist, "I know on the outside what she seems to be, but on the inside, I think she is just a frightened little girl," and he replied, "We think that too," but the sides warred continuously, and the little girl predominated rarely, and then only for a few days at a time.

It was summer, thankfully. I remember getting out of my vehicle, which I had parked in the mall's giant outside lot, readying myself to search for her, but not knowing what I would say if I found her, practising prevarication, the very prevarication at which she herself was so skilled, and there she was, not having seen me, but crossing the parking lot by herself, a worried frown on her face. Every few steps she would run to the back of a parked car and crouch down, gazing around in all directions as if someone dangerous were following her and she had to keep out of sight. But there was no one else in the parking lot at all.

When she saw me, she came straight over, and we spoke a little. I tried to get her to get into my car, but she was wary of me and refused. She started to walk away, that old look on her face, of complete dismissal of me or anyone else who tried to get her to do something she didn't want to do, her jaw set, her eyes fixed on that thing I couldn't see but that was the only power she answered to. I ran after her and caught her by the arm, importuning her to come with me, to let me help her, and when she tried to jerk away, I held on, even though she kept moving forward, dragging me.

I suddenly realized that I was the one committing a crime here — kidnapping or assault, I didn't know what. I let go of her arm, and watched her stride away toward the bus station. And yet, I think now in something close to wonder that she didn't try to hit me or trip me or push me away. She merely tried to disentangle herself from my grip, and so I let go, and watched her walk away. That might have been the last time I had her committed, but she had finally figured out that after a certain number of hours, maybe seventy-two, she didn't have to stay in the psychiatric ward, but could check herself out and walk away, although for the time being back on an even psychological keel. By then, with the medication she had been given, she would be back in balance mentally, at least for a while.

I always thought that I could explain things to her (things I didn't then understand myself), so that she would change what she chose. In the aftermath of one of her crises, when I'd driven five hours to collect her and straighten out whatever damage she had done to herself and others, and having no hotel room myself yet, and she having no home as a result of the crisis, we sat in my parked car near a suburban park, and I tried to say to her what I had never directly said, not in any general way before. I said, "All your life, since you were old enough to make choices yourself, you always chose to do exactly what you wanted to do, without regard to the needs or wants of anyone else. So now, I'm asking you, has it made you happy? Is your life a good one?" She didn't reply, had taken on the look of small, unhappy child again, sitting crumpled beside me. "Isn't it time you tried the way of the people who have tried to help you? Take your meds, go to a job every day, stay out of the bars and as far as possible away from the bikers and the pimps and the addicts and the just plain visibly vicious." (I probably didn't say that last part, but I was thinking it, and so was she.) She didn't reply. Of course, she had heard all this before.

This commitment was after her friend called me to report on her homelessness, and that she wasn't making any sense and was talking to people who weren't there, so that no one would let her stay with them. The friend said, "She's worn out her welcome everywhere." After that hospital stay, she had spent several months in a group home with a good woman running it, a religious woman, and with social workers and psychologists coming and going. During that time she had been meek and mild, and talked to me about the "girls" who resided there, too, and the fun things they did together, even going to church together, laughing in a natural, gentle way, and I could see that she really was trying my side of the line. At least for a while, although she might have been lying to me about the church-attendance, or how well she was getting along, as she was the most accomplished liar I've ever met. This hopeful interlude might have lasted three months and then she was gone again, walking out of the group home, not taking her meds, drinking — by then she was alcoholic — doing and/or selling drugs, and doing anything, including prostitution, she had to do to survive. She was in her early twenties then, and I think in that moment that I must have known that my case would never prevail.

I thought, we all thought, that when in her early thirties she finally married, we could step back, that her husband who loved her would take over. We had done our duty faithfully, as well as she would allow, and now she was in his hands. And he did take over: he, an indelibly hard worker in one of the construction trades, insisted that she get a job and go to work every single day; he took her to the medical people and had her sign documents that meant she consented to a monthly long-term injection, thereby eliminating the daily fight over taking her medication, and so, in his care, she stabilized. Then he died suddenly, a heart attack out of the blue when he was in his early forties. She phoned me, virtually incoherent, from the hospital, and of course, I came at once, located her, and together we went to their apartment where I would stay, I thought, to support her at least until the funeral was over.

She gave me the spare room that stank of old beer, and in which boxes of empty beer cans and bottles were piled wall to wall opposite the bed, up to the ceiling. She never got around to getting me a key for the building or her apartment, so I could only get in if she were with me. Then she went out drinking, with whom I didn't know, two nights in a row after his death. I woke early one morning, dampening down my fury, and knew the situation was hopeless. I moved out when she was still passed out on her bed in her clothes, and went to a hotel, not telling her which one. Although I spoke to her on the phone, I didn't see her until a day later at her husband's funeral, where she sat like a child, mute and limp in a flowery dress (or am I imagining that? Harking back to her pretty flocked white dress another relative had bought her for her Grade 8 grad, and how she had disappeared for an hour in the middle of the reception? Or was this just how I always saw her in my imagination — a frightened little girl?) In her best clothes, she sat waiting for the funeral to be over. I knew, we all knew, the second we heard the news, that soon she would be off her meds again, would abandon her job in a fast-food outlet, and before too long be on the street, and into drugs and alcohol, and eventually some prostitution to stay alive. It was after her husband died that she began running around the country, but only west, never east, calling me from distant cities, hallucinating or delusional or desperate for a place to stay.

And yet, I am completely aware of how very banal this story is, how commonplace, that it is said that many families have one — a "black sheep," that is — a representative of the chaos that our middle-class lifestyle is designed to hold at bay. As if all the promises we make to ourselves of the perfect peace and quiet comfort that will be ours if we just work hard enough and follow the rules, nothing like this will ever happen to us. So all our lives we work to hold back chaos, until we are forced to hold in our minds that chaos is as natural and right as is peace and stability, that we humans have to learn to strike a balance between the two forces pulling at us. That my young relative chose chaos, and kept choosing it no matter what happened, for her whole life, was always a huge puzzle to me. But I have said I know this situation to be commonplace, awful as it is, that all across this country many families struggle with family members who behave as if they hate their families, but who never finally cut ties, returning time and time again in search of help, only to take that help and disappear again until the next crisis occurs. Family after family, from the ones who give an intransigent teenager a few thousand dollars to go away and stay away, to those who somehow manage to strike a bargain with the teen about when they can come home and with whom and for how long they can stay, to those who, year after year, do what I and my family did: working for years to try to help. All of this, while society looks on and mostly (although pitying) condemns the families as "not being there" for the wayward kid or adult, never knowing that it is the wayward ones who refuse all rational help, and even if begged, will never stay in their own homes.

After her behaviour around the time of her husband's funeral, and her disregard, once again, this time of the several hundred miles I had driven to be with her, I didn't contact her, and she didn't contact me. She was into her mid-to-late thirties by now. I knew she had already abandoned her job and lost the apartment she had shared with her husband, and that if she wasn't on the street yet, she soon would be. For a couple of years, I didn't know where she was or what she was doing, no phone calls from the police, social workers, people who were trying to give her therapy, or anyone else from her life, and that interval gave me time to try to come to terms with what I would do the next time she phoned, as she absolutely would.

The phone call finally came in the early afternoon, but instead of her, it was a relative who had a heart condition and was gasping for breath, able to squeeze out only a few words at a time. He told me that I would have to handle the matter; he simply could not. This meant that the young relative had given up on me and carried this elderly relative's phone number with her instead of mine. The elderly relative gave me a phone number to call, that of a Mountie in a distant (although not that distant) city. The Mountie said that our young relative was dead. She was forty-two.

For years, we had told each other that she would be found dead in an alley, killed by one of the dangerous drug-and-alcohol-addled men she hung around with, or men as desperate as she was and maybe from the same cause or causes. None of us could say how she managed to escape that fate, perhaps because she was white, and because she was smart and had learned more about how to keep herself from traps and serious danger. That she died in traffic was both horrific and ironic.

Although I had decided never again to lift a finger on her behalf, I could hardly refuse this request from the sick relative who had phoned me. I didn't want to have to handle the matter of the disposition of her body or her funeral, nor the half-dozen times I could foresee before this matter was closed when I would have to tell her story to this official and that one. I dreaded this inevitable process. Even though I had loved her and over and over again tried to help her, I had begun at last to see myself not as a person who loved her, and whom she (somewhere deep down) loved, but as, simply, an enabler.

The Mountie told me that she had run out into traffic on a wide, although apparently not well-lit, street that was still busy at almost midnight, and had been hit by a car and thrown, then run over, by a second one. She had died four hours later in the emergency ward of a nearby hospital. By the time the Mountie in charge of her case and I connected, she had been dead for about twelve hours. Witnesses (who turned out to be the other drivers), the Mountie told me, said that she was alone, and that she did not carry so much as a purse with her.

One more time, it would be the last time, although I didn't think of that then, I spent most of a working day on the phone: calls to the hospital; to the hospital's morgue, where her body now was; calls to and from a social-work functionary of that provincial government to track down her record and her social insurance number, which nobody seemed to have, and which forced me to call the federal agency in charge of such numbers, who told me (as if it were a secret) that the only people who could legally get her number were police officers, which fact I then relayed to the social worker, who then told me she had already gotten it from the police. Obviously, she knew the process perfectly well, and trying to get me to find it was some bizarre impulse I don't understand. There were also calls to and from a funeral home and subsequent calls to other relatives to discuss what we should do with her remains. Then the calls were about her cremation and the decision to have her ashes shipped to me.

When I first heard the news, and for hours afterward, I had had every intention of going at once to the city where her body was, to see her and to make the arrangements in person, but when I told the funeral director that I would be there the next day, he seemed surprised and said that was hardly necessary, that everything could be done over the phone. It seemed clear to me that this was a situation he had dealt with often, and although it took me a while to come to the decision, which I felt guilty about at once and have never stopped feeling guilty over, I decided to take his advice and settle matters by telephone.

After a day or two of playing telephone tag, the coroner and I finally reached one another by telephone. At her request, one more time, I hoped the last forever, I began my young relative's story. Perhaps five or seven minutes in, the coroner interrupted me: "You don't need to go any further," she said. "I could tell you the same story about a young relative of mine. I know exactly what you are talking about."

She told me then that my young relative's blood alcohol count was so high, it was a wonder she could navigate, much less make a decision, that she had died four hours after the accident from head trauma and blood loss. She had been struck and run over late at night, but had died early the next day, on the birthday of my dead husband, who had also loved her.

Somewhere in there, after I had spoken for the first time with the Mountie, and then with the funeral home and various family members, my cellphone stopped working, although only for a few minutes; then my landline started making weird electronic noises, stopped functioning and then came back into use; the television set also went down for a while, and at the same time my computer started acting up. This all lasted perhaps six hours before things went back to normal. I took all the electronic malfunctioning as my now-deceased young relative's way of communicating the rage she still harboured toward me, as her way of letting me know that I wasn't forgiven for refusing and abandoning her.

These manifestations of her continuing fury toward me showed me only what I had always known when all was said and done, how pathetically powerless she was; how flailing out in rage, doing the most damage she could manage without regard to consequences for herself, was her only defense. I laughed a bit, but it was a rueful, sad laugh, and tears came to my eyes, but didn't fall. What I felt was not in my heart; it was in my soul, an ache for which there is no remedy. I think she must have had the same ineradicable ache that neither drugs nor alcohol nor sex nor money nor even the love of others had been able to do more than dampen, for a few minutes, a few hours, a few days. Then she swept on, pulled by that remorseless force, whatever it was, that she was in thrall to, a force we don't recognize, that seemed to come straight out of chaos. How could one not pity such a victim? Even while backing away.

Even though the Mounties had located the boyfriend from whom they said she had run that night, I was never able to ascertain if they had a room or an apartment or were staying in a shelter. He said she and her boyfriend had been fighting, but that was all, and I never so much as found out his name, or maybe I did and promptly forgot it. I believe he had her purse. That would have been how the Mountie had found the first relative who then phoned me and asked me to take over. I didn't pursue further information; she was dead, and I thought that would be pointless, but especially that it would be too painful to know any more about the last days of her life. It seemed to me that I already knew all too well how they would have been.

And, every time I thought of going in person to see her one last time, I thought of how her face would be so smashed as to be unrecognizable, and I did not want that last image of her to haunt me forever. But I know this was just an excuse for my last failure toward her. In the end, I abandoned her again. I think this was cruel, and a moral crime on my part; and yet, if I had to do it again, I think I would still choose not to go. I was exhausted with this narrative in my life and that of the rest of the family; I was not so much sickened, or guilt-ridden, or even angered, as I was worn out, and the inevitability of her too-early, violent death provided me with a degree of closure — even though I couldn't justify it to myself and still can't — that I chose to settle for.

I arranged a small funeral for her, announced her death and the time and place of the service in the newspaper in her city, and eventually had a headstone made and installed. Her former in-laws attended her funeral and perhaps four of her friends as well as myself and three other members of our family who lived nearby. A middle-aged male relative placed her urn that had been shipped to me in the ground, a pastor said some prayers, and her life on earth was over. The next day, I came back to my home city. Weeks later, it came to me with certainty that her running into traffic was not a drunken mistake. It was suicide.

I could keep on telling this story all night and into tomorrow morning, but the end is always the same: She and I disagreed on the definition of "saved," neither of us able to accept the other's definition, and now she is dead. I have not heard from her since those few hours when all my electronic equipment went haywire at once and I chose to think she had caused it. I don't even dream of her, and I wonder what that means more than I would wonder if I dreamed of her night after night, as I do with my other much-loved dead. Of my failure to stay with her on her journey, I alternate between guilt and anger, but mostly, I feel what I always have: bafflement and a long and deep sorrow.

ON THE PANDEMIC
May 28, 2020

It's the oddest thing, like something out of Kafka or some other long-dead austere dystopian writer, as I sit alone in my condo in near-perfect health, breathing the same fresh air on my balcony as I always have, gazing at the same peaceful view I've been gazing at for ten years, that out there, beyond the rim of the horizon, in every direction, people are dying. They are dying in the hundreds, then the thousands, comatose for days, or in great physical agony and mostly alone. Alone, while their families sit by the phone waiting for news, or in vigil on the sidewalk outside the building, where in some anonymous room the beloved is dying, or already dead, they don't know, and no one answers the phone or calls to those waiting in anguish for news.

Starting with videos out of Wuhan, China, the news is appalling: We see a man wearing a black business suit lying neatly on the street, dead — we can only speculate that in the night someone put him there — then we see a smuggled cellphone video of a Chinese hospital with bodies lying on the floor so thickly there is no room to walk among them, and staff in virtual hysterics. From there, we begin to see our own less congested but still frantic hospitals, their exhausted staff, sometimes in tears, always deeply worried ("People are dying in ways that . . . just aren't normal," a young doctor says, holding back tears), and rows of comatose people in ICUs attached to arrays of tubes, and looking like something out of any one of a dozen organ-theft thriller movies.

We grow more and more frightened, or maybe horrified is the truer word. We know we're supposed to be scared enough that we'll do what we're told is best, but for most of us, that level of terror is hard to maintain for own lives and those of our loved ones, when outside our windows no ambulances race past, there are no sobbing people, no one coughing or vomiting or staggering by calling out for help, no bodies lying in the streets, no SWAT teams dragging kicking, screaming people out of their homes. Only the same wide playing fields, the schools with their empty asphalt playgrounds, the rows of small houses sitting quietly as they always have, and the rare person walking casually by, usually with a leashed dog.

Personally, I can't reconcile the two realities. I keep waiting for them to fit together in a simultaneous whole, and even though I keep the isolation and distancing rules and go to the grocery store once a week and otherwise go out only for a daily walk, alone and in my neighbourhood, the disconcerting companion fact is that I don't know anyone who is sick, or even anyone who knows someone who is sick, much less has died. With everyone else, I listen to the radio and watch newscast after newscast on television switching among Canadian and American channels, and then adding the BBC and then Al Jazeera, trying to grasp the enormity and, especially, the pertinacity to me of the crisis. I find it an effort not to succumb to the always — if vaguely — threatening fear that it will all end in food riots, lootings, and the appearance of roving bands of zombie killers. We're Canadians, we tell ourselves; maybe in the USA, but never here. Or those of us, like me, more inclined to skepticism than to hysteria, steel ourselves against the impulse to just ignore the whole business and go to the mall. Except that the mall is closed, even the library is closed, nor can we get on a plane and vanish to reemerge on a beach in Mexico or Australia, or to wander in awe through cathedrals in Spain or temples in Cambodia. *It* is everywhere; like a more noxious Christmas, you can't avoid it.

Even as I listen most mornings to our prime minister's cool, rational and more or less decisive speeches delivered without a second's hesitation or any quibbles, it seems to me that the truth is that confusion reigns, and, in fact, that there are no experts on Covid-19. I'm one among many who thinks that the figures we see every day on our TV screens can't be entirely accurate; on occasion they even differ as I flip back and forth between channels; the infection ratio goes up and then down, and who knows, somewhere in the distant future, what it will turn out to really have been. The same is true of the mortality rate — it is or it isn't whatever number science is currently providing, which also changes with the constantly changing data coming in from around the world. And still, I am one of many who knows no one who is ill, and, certainly, no one who has died.

I feel a bit like those people who refuse to believe that astronauts ever walked on the moon. "Cognitive dissonance," we used to say, or "Does — Not — Compute," in robot voices, rolling our eyes around in their sockets. Despite this unease, though, like most other people's, my greatest fear is to find myself responsible for somebody else's death, so, discretion being the better part of valour, I too keep on distancing and isolating, even as many of us who live alone are wondering which would happen first: the gradual lessening of the lockdown, or our complete descent into insanity. I wonder, does the government have an algorithm to tell them when to let up, so as not to have too many crazed Jeremiahs striding, shouting through the neighbourhoods? I can't help but wonder what the American humourist and essayist David Sedaris is writing about it all. And also, what devastating and original — if slightly dubious — insight Susan Sontag would have, if she were alive.

As for me, even though near-total isolation gives you a lot of time to think, I haven't been able to come up with a single original thing to say about our situation, and still can't. But, during this time, I have had confirmed for me something I've never positively been sure of, that I am indeed an introvert: life in lockdown isn't all that much different for me than it was before lockdown. Although, as time passes, my solitary life without so much as a single break for lunch, coffee or a movie with even one friend, weighs on me as it never has before. By last week, when Mother's Day rolled around, my interior fuming, which up to that point I'd either not noticed or successfully squelched, was getting pretty hard to keep tamped down.

Personally, I suspect that governments are putting on their game faces for the daily report, believing it essential to appear in full control, with gentle wisdom leaking out of their ears. One of my early suspicions, that mostly the leaders don't know what they're talking about, has morphed into wondering how much of this is true of their pronouncements about just about everything, in a general way, through at least my entire life going back to my birth in propaganda-saturated wartime. Uh-oh. Better not go there. Democracy only works, when you think about it, because of the populace's willing suspension of disbelief, a term coined by Samuel Taylor Coleridge, originally referring to how fiction works.

And as for scientists, I don't entirely trust them, either. I'm remembering Joseph Lister (1827–1912) who, around 1865, developed his germ theory, and who thus recommended handwashing and cleanliness in surgical suites and at childbirth in order to lessen the horrific death rates in both places. For this certainty, he was nearly hounded out of his profession by his colleagues. In the time of Covid-19, need I point out the additional irony? Although, it must be said that I don't for a second doubt scientists' goodwill, nor their desperate desire to solve this problem for the benefit of humankind. As time passes, despite the best efforts of science, though, the death toll around the world rises and rises again and keeps rising. Bubonic plague killed off something like one-third of Europe in the fourteenth century; Spanish flu killed around fifty million people worldwide in 1918; we can avoid such atrociously high numbers, they tell us, if we just do what's asked.

I don't know anybody who refuses to obey the new guidelines, although I think there might be some sneaking around after dark. I have witnessed in my own neighbourhood, a couple of times, groups of people in yards or on the sidewalk chatting and laughing together, standing too close to each other, as if it's normal times. What is more common in my admittedly always tiny little world (growing smaller by the minute) is news of acquaintances going overboard with the restrictions, far beyond what we're asked to do or not do, busily ramping up their own fears, and growing not less, but more, cautious by the moment, until a true paranoia sets in. When asked, they admit for the most part, like me, to knowing no one who is even ill, and eventually at least not seriously ill, and certainly nobody who has died. It seems to me that for them, Covid-19 has taken on the weight of all the things one fears in life, now cohering into an enormous, amorphous shadow spreading relentlessly down the streets and through the neighbourhoods, growing bigger by the moment, and more threatening and dangerous, so that merely opening the front door will bring on The End.

Well, no use second-guessing the country's leaders or the scientists, from medical doctors to microbiologists to virologists, epidemiologists, and infectious disease specialists. But a little healthy disrespect and questioning strikes me as always prudent. We have a combination of nobody knowin' nuthin' as the saying goes, except that if you get sick and are one of the vulnerable, if you live, you will still go through weeks and weeks of the most awful misery, and at least in some cases never be the same again, and a faintly dismal, but firm, recitation by leaders across the country of the numbers sick and numbers dead all delivered with apparent sincerity and certainty. It is as if they have all practised behind the scenes about how best to present themselves and their material to avoid rousing the public into catcalls and disobedience of the protocols laid out for them. In this, the media also, one suspects, tutored as well, cooperate fully, so that whatever device you turn on for information you get more or less the same message. Over and over and over again. Only in the unruly United States, with its divide-and-rule and anything-goes-if-it-works-for-me president are some people objecting, and putting up a fight, and questioning what the hell is going on. A few of them, anyway, although there is apparently a relatively tiny protest or two in Canada that somebody told me about. News of that sort of thing is bound to be limited. The huge hardship the restrictions — no gatherings, distancing, isolation — impose on a large segment of the population (barely counteracted by the daily ministerial announcements of limited financial help for one sector and then another), also serve to keep people docile. Don't get me wrong: I know this plague to be deadly, that we have to do what we can to stop it. If I could do math, I would here estimate today's equivalent, adjusted for today's much greater population, of the fifty-million-dead figure of 1918.

I sit at home alone, watching television, and think these thoughts and wonder if I said them out loud, would I be lynched, declared a danger to the public, and have my laptop taken away, or imprisoned? Or if I'm merely crazy, a state, as most of my circle knows anyway, I've never been that far from at the best of times. After all, these measures are for the best, I tell myself, these people are trying to save our lives, and without a vaccine or a cure, what else might they do? We all wonder what will happen in Sweden with its mere ten million people, a country that hasn't gone into total lockdown. I think it's impossible to know yet if they're right or wrong, but pockets of non-Swedish citizens (and a few Swedish citizens) are adamant either that Swedish authorities are reckless and suicidal, or that they're the only sensible leaders in the world. So far — May 2020 — Sweden's figures of the ill and the dead without the standard lockdown aren't as good as their neighbours, but are nowhere near as bad as countries who chose lockdown predict or merely fear. A novelist, I can't help but imagine a scenario in which the world's leaders got together to discuss what was best to do about the pandemic, and Sweden volunteered to be the guinea pig, the baseline country in a massive experiment to provide data to prove or disprove the necessity of lockdown measures. Sweden: a cold country, still mostly Protestant, predominately white, educated, democratic, socialist, rational in politics and life, and non-effusive in social style. I've no idea what any of those factors have to do with the pandemic, but then nobody else does either.

Four months away from my eightieth birthday, though, I can hardly avoid noticing that something like eighty per cent of deaths in our own country (I read this morning the percentage was closer to ninety), are of those elderly who live in one kind or another of long-term care facility. That is, those with dementia, and those who suffer from the ailments of the old: heart disease, severe arthritis, the consequences of strokes, high blood pressure, and other chronic diseases such as Parkinson's, diabetes, lung disease, ALS, and multiple sclerosis. Mostly, but not entirely, those who have "pre-existing conditions" and thus are more susceptible. With our economy long ago set up so that both parents have to have jobs to survive financially, no one is left at home to care for the elderly, or in many cases including my own, nobody left at home at all. Citizens, without deliberately setting out to think that way, got the idea that the elderly are too much trouble, can't reasonably be managed by family members and that "care homes" were the solution to the problem of the useless, inconvenient, and troublesome old. Not to deny that the old — given the way our society is organized — are inconvenient, often troublesome, and mostly (as far as most of the younger can figure out) not of much use to anybody. And nobody knows that prevailing attitude better than the shamed and helpless old. Family members, more ready to bear the burden of the cost of such care than to quit a job to stay at home with the elder, or simply not knowing how to care for the profoundly compromised, put their trust in these facilities, indeed, are urged to put their trust in them. It would seem now that this trust is often, although far from always, misplaced, and, in some notorious cases, massively so. Protections for the elderly in these facilities were too often simply not there, and management too often failed abysmally to take appropriate steps or take them quickly enough as the pandemic approached.

Blame has gone immediately to the fact that jobs in care homes are very poorly paid, and part-time, that to earn enough to live, employees have to work in several homes, thus carrying all manner of viruses and germs from facility to facility. For most part, these factors are the source of the inexcusable number of deaths of the elderly in certain care homes. Not to mention that many care homes, as with schools, simply have gotten far too large. "Warehousing" as people say; the elderly put in such places to wait for death. Although it is absolutely true that the bulk of employees in such places could use more training, and certainly that doing such important work for close to the lowest pay our society offers anybody is unconscionable. It is also true that if you are overworked and underpaid, you have little incentive except your own human-ity to do a good job. But I resist the simplicity of blaming those failures and ensuing deaths on so easy a target. What is more to blame is the lack of adequate funding for care homes, at least the public ones — and this fact is a measure of what we think of the elderly whose only choice is to live in these places. It is pretty clear, too, that the privatizing of long-term care homes, where the major motive is profit rather than humani-tarian concerns, followed by the failure of governments to ensure adequate, timely inspections of these places, is and was a recipe for the disaster that has — inevitably — occurred.

Of course, it always behooves an essayist to tell the other side of the story, or at least to point in that direction. Not all care homes are underserved with employees, not all have the virus running rampant through them, and not all of the elderly living in such places are incompetent, neglected, and miserable. Some, indeed, if in the right facility (usually but not always involving quite a bit of money) are better off than sitting alone in an empty house or apartment with no companionship at all, the television on from morning to night, and no one to pick up the elderly person if he/she falls, or has a stroke, or starts to bleed copiously from one orifice or another, no one to phone for help, if said elder can't get to the phone. In these facilities, some of the elderly perk up, take an interest in living again, and their health and outlook on life improves with regular care, various expert therapies, and the steady vigilance of staff. But mostly, and I am an elder and my friends are too, the day of the move to the care home is the saddest day of one's last years. (Even a friend living in such a place disputes this last opinion, but I hold firm, and remind people that "de Nile" ain't just a river in Egypt.)

And yet, another friend, who pays a private home a large amount of money per month to live there, seems to have zero control over what management decrees, and refers to the administration as "they," implying her own helplessness. Loss of control over one's life is what the old seem to dread the most, and, as long as they are able, rail the most against, even to the extent of choosing to live in ways that seem to be entirely against their own best interests. Meaning, of course, the aged couldn't possibly know what their own best interests are. The deaths of so many of the elderly in long-term care institutions doesn't just indicate a shortage of love for the aged and infirm, but a fundamental lack of respect for them; at worst, a disbelief in their humanity. It seems to me that this determination by the non-elderly is a consequence of the death-denying culture in which we live, where youth is overvalued, the middle-aged control the world, and the old are perceived as useless and, therefore, better dead. What we need is a cultural shift, the components of which would have to start with valuing the old and infirm so as to give them the best, rather than the worst, during the last period of life.

Of course, the elderly should be valued more, and deserve to be cared for, if their families won't or can't, by trained people, and such people should be paid more than barely adequate wages to do so. And of course, to rail against the entire system of caring for the elderly as they enter that last period of life, from those who go into apartments in assisted-living buildings, to those lost in advanced dementias going into locked wards, to those who, though mentally sound, are physically unable to care for themselves, I admit smacks of simple rage rather than reasoned argument. But paying people more to do an inadequate job of caring for the elderly is not a solution in itself. It's the barest beginning, and right now seems like locking the barn door after the horse is gone.

And now, this pandemic. How to write original thoughts in a situation about which so few solid facts are known? I feel that the best I can do is to rely on my personal experience: even though I am in the almost worst-hit category (aged but with no underlying conditions), I have chosen to buy my own groceries, on the grounds that it isn't ethical or even moral for me to put somebody else at risk to get them for me when I am capable in every way of getting them myself. There is also the factor that I don't hear anybody mentioning: that not all of us want to live forever, that some or possibly a good percentage of the old would prefer to check out rather than spend the last few years in a state of steady but unrelenting decline, the numbers of medication one takes constantly climbing, the decrepitude advancing inexorably, the spectre of some degree of dementia looming, as well as blindness and/or deafness, and then the weeks, months, or even years of lying helpless in a long-term care home or being a burden on some younger family member. I have the right to live if I choose to, no matter what, but I also believe I have the right not to. Accordingly, I am willing to take my chances at the grocery store.

Lest people object to my reckless risking of illness and perhaps burdening the not-so-abundant health care system in a time of crisis, when it is needed for those unfortunate people who took no silly risks: I have a Personal Consent form already filled out and signed and hanging on my fridge which says, Do Not Resuscitate, and do not take any heroic measures to save my life. I won't be using a ventilator, thank you, and even though I've heard that a Covid-19 death is a most ugly one unless one is rendered comatose, I'll take comatose and just check out without using up those precious resources. And yet I have to apologize and explain? Such is the effect of the rampant ageism in our society.

To quote from the letter sent by Margaret Gillis (President of the International Longevity Centre Canada) and Kiran Rabheru (Board Chair ILC Canada) to the prime minister and the opposition leaders in Canada's House of Commons, dated April 17, 2020:

> *We are writing to express our abhorrence at the egregious mistreatment of older people in Canada and around the world during the COVID 19 pandemic. This global crisis has clearly demonstrated the very real lethal impact of ageism on the fundamental human rights of older people as evidenced by: the appalling mistreatment of older Canadians in Long-term Care; systematic and severe restrictions to health care, resulting in the culling of older persons in Italy; and the treatment of older people in the press and social media as evidenced by the trending phrase "Boomer Remover."*

As per the adage, "what you permit, you promote",
any country that permits human rights violations
needs to be held accountable. It is urgent and imperative
that Canada take definitive action to lead the world
in upholding fundamental human rights, something
our nation is so well respected for historically.
We are demanding that the Canadian Government
take immediate and decisive steps toward leading and
supporting a United Nations (UN) Convention on the
Rights of all Older Persons.

With the opinions expressed in these paragraphs and with the rest of the letter, I concur absolutely.

We're all wondering too, what the world will be like post-Covid-19. Some speculate that the world will be vastly different: air travel again only affordable for the rich; international tourism nearly dead; globalism a tenth of what it was; pollution drastically lowered; and so on. Personally, I think things will slowly go back to generally the way they used to be. "Generally" being me hedging my bets. There will always be among us those greedy for power or money or both, and the cruel and the venal, just as there will always be the gentle, the kind, the wise. Covid-19 will slow the world down for a while, enabling a reset as things start to ramp up again, but I think only in pockets and in various procedures and institutions will there be any real, permanent change.

The failure in humanity — the failure of a civilization — concerning the elderly upon whom Covid-19 has opened the curtain must be one of those traumatic recognitions that result in that real, permanent change. We aged, and those who love us, wait for the frequent condescending and unkind attitudes and inadequate and often inappropriate arrangements for us to be replaced by respectful, cooperative, generous, and sensitive treatment, and also, for the recognition of the gifts of imagination that come with only with age.

BBC, "16-24 year olds are the loneliest age group according to new BBC Radio 4 survey," *BBC Media Centre* (October 1, 2018), https://www.bbc.co.uk/mediacentre/latestnews/2018/loneliest-age-group-radio-4.

Thomas Dumm, *Loneliness as a Way of Life* (Cambridge, Mass.: Harvard U Press, 2008).

Franklin Foer, *World Without Mind: The Existential Threat of Big Tech* (New York: Penguin/Random House, 2017).

Frieda Fromm-Reichmann, "Loneliness," *Psychiatry* 22 (1959), 1–15.

Yuval Noah Harari, *Sapiens: A Brief History of Humankind* (Israel: Dvir Publishing House Ltd, 2011; In English: New York: Harper, 2015).

Amanda Hess, "Race, Class, and the Stigma of Riding the Bus in America," *Bloomberg CityLab* (July 10, 2012), https://www.bloomberg.com/news/articles/2012-07-10/race-class-and-the-stigma-of-riding-the-bus-in-america.

James Hillman, *The Force of Character: And the Lasting Life* (New York: Random House, 1999).

James Hollis, *Finding Meaning in the Second Half of Life: How to Finally, Really Grow Up* (New York: Penguin Group, 2005).

Jacques Lusseyran, *And There Was Light* (New York: Parabola Books, 1999).

Michel de Montaigne, "On Solitude," *The Complete Essays of Montaigne* (Stanford, CA: Stanford University Press, 1957).

Online Etymology Dictionary: www.etymonline.com.

Oxford English Dictionary: The Compact Edition, (Oxford: Oxford University Press, 1981).

Roszak, Theodore, *America the Wise: The Longevity Revolution and the True Wealth of Nations* (New York: Houghton Mifflin, 1998).

Judith Shulevitz, "The Science of Loneliness: How Isolation Can Kill You," *The New Republic* (May 12, 2013), https://newrepublic.com/article/113176/science-loneliness-how-isolation-can-kill-you.

Sir Philip Sidney, *Arcadia* (1586), http://www.luminarium.org/renascence-editions/arcadia1.html (accessed February 28, 2021).

Anthony Storr, *Solitude: A Return to the Self* (New York: The Free Press, 1988).

World Health Organization, "Control and prevention of blindness and deafness: who releases new global estimates on visual impairment," *World Health Organization: Regional Office for the Eastern Mediterranean* (April 18, 2012), http://www.emro.who.int/control-and-preventions-of-blindness-and-deafness/announcements/global-estimates-on-visual-impairment.html.

ACKNOWLEDGEMENTS

"Against Ageism" appeared in a slightly different form in
The Walrus, April 2018.

"Storage" was published in *Waiting: An Anthology of Essays*,
edited by Rona Altrows and Julie Sedivy (Edmonton:
University of Alberta Press, 2018).

"This Strange Visible Air" is from a short speech delivered
in Saskatoon, Winnipeg, and Regina at a 2017 series,
"Nature Talks" organized and sponsored by the Nature
Conservancy of Canada.

"Perceptible Light" is published in *You Look Good for Your Age*,
edited by Rona Altrows (Edmonton: University of Alberta
Press, 2021).

"Open Your Eyes," appeared in *The Walrus* in a different form,
in 2021.

I'd like to thank my agent, Marilyn Biderman, of Transatlantic
Agency for her careful reading of these essays, and Naomi K.
Lewis for her excellent, meticulous editing.

SHARON BUTALA, an Officer of the Order of Canada, is the award-winning author of twenty-one books of fiction and nonfiction and five produced plays. She has three times been a finalist for the Governor General's Literary Award, and is a recipient of the Marian Engel Award, the Saskatchewan Order of Merit, the Cheryl and Henry Kloppenburg Award for Literary Excellence, and the City of Calgary W.O. Mitchell Book Prize. She lives in Calgary.

sharonbutala.com